JN409280

Poems of 100 Major Contemporary Korean Poets

Translated by Chang-Soo Ko

한국 대표 100인 영역시선

Poems of 100 Major Contemporary
Korean Poets

Translated by
Ko Chang-su

다시올

TRANSLATORS NOTE

This anthology includes the works of major poets active in the contemporary Korean literary scene. Most of them belong to a group of poets called the Dasiall literary group, who are both firmly rooted in Korean poetic traditions and at the same time forward-looking in their outlook. Translating Korean poetry into a medium so different linguistically such as the English language is an extremely difficult task. Poetic and cultural elements like rhythm, metaphor, and lyrical and musical qualities are often distorted or otherwise damaged in the process of translation into another language. While being faithful to the content and form of the original poem, the translator ought to make his/her best efforts to produce readable poetry in the target language.

Translated by **Chang-Soo Ko**

서문

이 영역시집에는 한국 시단에서 활동하고 있는 원로 시인을 포함하여 중요한 현역시인들의

작품이 실려있다. 포함된 시인의 대부분은 한국 시 전통에 튼실하게 뿌리를 두면서도 미래지향적인 시인들의 모임인 다시올문학회에서 활동하는 시인이다. 한국 시를 언어적으로 동떨어진 영어라는 매체로 번역하는 일은 극히 어려운 작업인바, 운율, 음악성, 은유, 서정성 같은 시적, 문화적 요소들은 다른 언어로 번역되는 과정에서 왜곡되거나 손상되는 경우가 많다. 번역자는 원시의 내용과 표현에 충실하면서도 대상언어로 읽기 쉬운 시가 되도록 최선을 다해야 할 것으로 안다.

번역 **고창수**

chapter 01

chapter 02

chapter 03

chapter 04

Ko Chang-su_I Yeong-sik_Gim Dong-ho

Bae In-hwan_O Se-yeong_Yu An-jin_Moon Jeong-hee

I geon cheong_Mun In-su_I mu won_I Geon-seon_Gim Du-hwan

Song Hi-bok_Gim Jeong-yun_Gim Gi-san

Bak Seung-mi_Hwang Gyeong-sik_Jeong Il-geun

Bae Chang-hwan_I Eun-bong

Jang Seok-nam_Gong Goeng-gyu

Bak Nam-hui_Bak Jeong Dae_Pak Mi-ra

Ma Gyeong-deok

Poems of 100 Major
Contemporary Korean Poets

chapter 01

Ko Chang-su_I Yeong-sik_Gim Dong-ho

Bae In-hwan_O Se-yeong_Yu An-jin_Moon Jeong-hee

I geon cheong_Mun In-su_I mu won_I Geon-seon_Gim Du-hwan

Song Hi-bok_Gim Jeong-yun_Gim Gi-san

Bak Seung-mi_Hwang Gyeong-sik_Jeong Il-geun

Bae Chang-hwan_I Eun-bong

Jang Seok-nam_Gong Goeng-gyu

Bak Nam-hui_Bak Jeong Dae_Pak Mi-ra

Ma Gyeong-deok

Mohenjo-Daro

Ko Chang-su

So we take over from your poets
The interrupted, broken stones they wove on your looms
To carry on their narratives.
This is the meaning of myth and history.

We draw our drinking water from your dried wells.
Water and fire nourish and punish civilization.
Let your eternally dead shift from granite gaze
Back to the flames of time-space
Alive with vision and voice, greed and grace.

Mohenjo-Daro,
We celebrate and glorify the day
When man first looked at the world
Through your eyes.
We celebrate the day when man first recognized
His own heartbeat as cosmic pulses.
We are here to cultivate our love for
Darkness and ignorance.
We are here to cultivate your light and darkness
In your most secret places.
We are here to meditate on our sole heritage,
The mystery of being and unbeing.

The geography of your towns,
Your skeletons and water mills,
All move towards some benevolent end
As our hands and faces move
Towards some benevolent hands that will receive them
At the end of time.

모헨조다로

고 창 수

그리하여 우리는 그대의 시인들이
그대의 물레로 짠
끊기고 깨어진 이야기들을 이어받아
그들의 서사시를 이어간다.

이는 바로 신화와 역사가 지니는 의미이다.
우리는 그대의 마른 우물에서 마실 물을 퍼올 린다.
물과 불은 문명을 키우고 벌한다.
그대의 영영 죽은 자들을 화강암의 응시에서 일깨워
환상과 목소리, 탐욕과 은혜가 살아 있는
시공의 불길 속으로 시선을 돌리게 하라.

모헨조다로여!
우리는 처음으로 사람이 그대의 눈으로
세상을 바라본 날을
기념하고 송축한다.
우리는 사람이 처음으로
제 심장의 고동이 우주의 맥박임을
깨달은 날을 송축한다.
우리는 지금 여기에서
어둠과 무명에 대한 우리의 사랑을 가꾸려 이곳에 왔다.
우리는 그대의 가장 은밀한 곳에서 그대의 빛과 어둠을 가꾸러 이곳에 왔다.

우리의 유일한 유산인
있고 없음의 이 신비를 명상하려고
우리는 이곳에 왔다.

마치 우리의 손과 얼굴이
시간이 끝나는 날 그들을 받아줄
어떤 자비로운 손길을 향하여 움직여 가듯,
그대 도시의 지리와
그대의 화석 뼈와 물레방아들은 모두
어떤 자비로운 목적지를 향하여 가고 있다.

POME

고창수
1965년~1966년 《시문학》등단. 1965년 영국문화원 주최 Shakespeare Short Story Contest에 영문 단편소설 입선. 1965년-1996년 주이디오피아대사, 주시애틀총영사, 국제문화협력대사, 주파키스탄대사 역임. 1976년 시집 『파편 줍는 노래』 외 11권, 1980년 한국문학번역상 수상, 현 다시올문학 편집고문

Dasiall Path – Return–again Path

I Yeong–sik

On the fringe of Mount Bukhan
There is a lovely hidden path that
each morning forms new dew
and opens the forest with the soul' s first steps.
The Dasiall path, the Return–again Path;
Once you sink into it,
you look for a way to come back again.
A place where
the squirrel, having hidden away a chestnut,
and now missing its own nest,
asks the passerby about the way.
A place that gently nurses the hardest wound
with the shade of the bush path.
The silence is profound as if it could revive the voice
of the dead bird.
The wild flower in the stump field blooms
season after season,
waiting for the day of your return.
Writers, calligraphers and painters!
Come with your naked body
to the Dasiall path;

we' ll build a bridge
with the bones of the wind
over the wasteland lacking artistic spirit.

Come back again,
Harboring love in your eyes and heart.

다시올레길

이 영 식

북한산 끝자락
아침마다 새 이슬 빚어
영혼의 첫발자국으로 숲을 열어 주는
착한 길 숨어 있습니다
한번 스며들고 나면
또다시 올 궁리부터 찾게 되는
다시올길

알밤 숨겨놓은 다람쥐가
제 구멍 놓치고
길손에게 길을 묻는 곳
파벽돌 같은 상처도
잡목림 그늘로 서늘히 감싸 주는 곳
죽은 새소리도 살려낼 듯
고요 깊습니다

등걸밭 야생화 절기절기 피어
그대 올 날 기다리노니
글쟁이, 먹쟁이, 그림쟁이여
맨몸뚱이로 오시라
다시올레길

예술혼 궁벽한 허무 위에
바람 뼈로 다리를 놓아 드리겠습니다

눈엔 듯 가슴엔 듯
사랑인 듯 품고 다시 오시라

POME
이영식
경기도 이천 출생
2000년 《문학사상》 등단
시집 『공갈빵이 먹고 싶다』 『희망온도』 『휴休』
lys-poem@hanmail.net

? LOVE SONG

Gim Dong-ho

The claws of a large crane
Unloading huge cinders,
How can they be so soft
More tender than our child's cute little hands?

The mole has sharp claws
That trowel the earth.
The woodpecker an elaborate bill
That drills through the wood's bark.
Man has gentle questions
That gouge the genesis of existence.

? has the shape of ice becoming pearls of water
A sorrowful shape melting into tear drops.
The shape of O's skein of thread as it unravels

People enjoy their own conclusions:
enjoy terminating the universe with one dot (.).
But there are things that open as soon as they close.
?..?..?..
Is ? then the biggest key on earth?

Of an evening I was bent on a late-night search
For a butterfly with four paws and
Silvery patterns resembling
? under its rear wings,
So in a dream
I put on a pair of tinted glasses
Riddled with holes upon holes.

? 戀歌

김 동 호

큰 짐 하역하는 대형 크레인의 손가락이
어쩌면 저리도 보드라울까
우리 아기 고사리 손 보다도 더 보드랍네

두더지에겐 땅을 파는 날카로운 발톱이 있다
딱따구리에겐 나무결을 파는 정교한 부리가 있다
사람에겐 존재의 근원을 파는 보드라운 물음이 있다

어름이 녹아 물방울 되는 모습, ?의 모양이다
슬픔이 녹아 눈물방울 되는 모습, ?의 모양이다
0의 실타래 막- 풀어지기 시작하는 모습, ?의 모양이다

사람들은 한 點 종지부로 우주를 닫기를 좋아한다
그러나 닫기가 무섭게 여는 것이 있으니 ?. ?. ?.
?은 지상최대의 열쇠일까

네발나비, 뒷날개 아래쪽에
? 모양의 은빛 무늬가 있다 해서
밤늦게까지 찾고 찾던 날 밤
나는 꿈속에서 구멍 숭숭 난 색안경을 썼다

POME
김동호
1975년 《현대시학》 등단, 군포문인협회 회장 역임, 공간시낭동회 회장 역임
성균관대학교 명예교수, 다시올문학 편집고문, 성균문학상, 2007년 시인들이 뽑는 시인상 수상, 시집 『꽃』『시산일기』『五弦琴』『배꼽음반』 외 6권
kimdongho66@hanmail.net

After a Journey to Mexico

Bae In-hwan

I saw only stones,
Reckless stone structures.
I saw numberless carvings in stone.
Somehow I felt sad
Though they highly praised the art of stone.

Water was nothing other than life,
Rain was nothing other than mercy.
Temples were a necessity;
Human sacrifice was a necessity, too.

The notion that gods loved blood;
There was always blood in the ruler's head.

Skulls were excavated
in Teotihuacan
in Monte Alban
in Palenque Ruin
in Uxmal
and in Chichen Itza.

Numberless skulls were discovered;

Skulls are speaking.

멕시코 여행을 마치고

배 인 환

돌만 보았다
무모에 가까운 석축물
돌에 새겨진 무수한 조각을 보았다.
돌의 예술이라고 극찬을 하는데
왠지 서글픈 생각이 든다.

물은 곧 생명이고
비는 곧 자비였다
신전은 필연이었다
인신 공양도 필연이었다

신은 피를 좋아한다는 발상
통치자의 머리에는 늘 피가 있었다.

떼오띠우아칸Teotihuacan에도
몬떼 알반Monte Alban에도
빨렌께 유적Palenque Ruin에도
우쉬말Uxmal에도
치첸 잇싸Chichen Itza에서도
해골이 발굴되었다.

무수히 많은 해골이 발견되었다.
해골이 말하고 있다.

POME

배인환
《현대시학》 등단
저서 김구용평전 『완화초당의 그리움』, 시집 『외눈 안경알』 『가장밝은 시간』 외 3권
영역 시선집『Poems of In-Hwan Bac』, 수필집 『아버지의 원두막과 어머니의 유품』 외 3권, 성균관문학상수상

Live by the Word

O Se-yeong

Man lives
not by bread
but by the Word.
Living means moving by oneself.
As the locomotive acquires motor power
by burning coal, diesel or gas,
the body gets its energy from bread;
the soul lives by the Word.
Noise, din, roar, explosion, sounds of wind, dead leaves
or waves...
This world overflows with all kinds of sounds,
but His low voice softly whispers to my ears.
The heat efficiency of words
that at times move us to cry
make us groan with a shudder
or make us laugh with compunction.
Is it clean fuel?
The ash of words that remain from the burning
within my ears;
I pick my ears.

말씀으로 산다

오 세 영

인간은
빵으로 사는 것이 아니라
말씀으로 산다.
산다는 것은 스스로 움직인다는 것
기차가
석탄을, 디젤을, 가스를 태워
동력을 얻듯
육신은 빵에서 에너지를 구하지만 영혼은
말씀으로 산다.
잡음, 소음, 굉음, 폭음, 바람소리, 갈잎소리, 파도소리……
이 세상은 온통 소리들로 넘쳐나는데
내 귀에 살며시 입을 대고 속삭이는 그의
낮은 음성.
때로는 감동으로 울리고,
때로는 전율로 신음케 하고,
때로는 자책으로 웃기는 말들의
그 열효율熱效率.
청정 연료일까.
내 귀속에서 연소하다 남은
말씀의 재,
귓밥을 판다.

POME

오세영
《현대문학》 등단. 시집으로 『시간의 뗏목』 『봄은 전쟁처럼』 『문열어라 하늘아』
학술서 『20세기 한국시 연구』 『상상력과 논리』 『우상의 눈물』 『문학과 그 이해』 등
소월시문학상, 정지용 문학상, 만해상 문학부문 대상, 시협상 등 수상
poetoh@naver.com

Glaucoma

Yu An-jin

The soldiers to whom I've sent consolation letters
looked like lovers or younger brothers
but now look like youngest sons.

As if the world looked white as with snow,
each age group gets cataract operations.
In my eyes somehow people who appear
on newspapers or broadcast programs
emerge with eyes, nose, mouth, ears all too blue.

As if eye mucus and eyelashes became
May's grass field or
a riverside thick with wet fog.
Green skirts noisily flutter
over hills where fleecy clouds used to drift quietly.
Yeah, yeah!
One surely eats the age.
One's age is eaten and digested like that.
The world ever gets younger.
Certainly it not only gets younger but childlike.

녹내장

유 안 진

위문편지를 써 보냈던 국군 아저씨들이
연인처럼 보이다가
동생처럼 보이다가
어느 새 막내아들 같은데

세상이 눈 덮힌 듯 하얗게 보이는지
또래마다 백내장白內障이라고 눈수술을 하는데
내 눈에는 왠지 신문에 방송에 나오는 분들도
눈 코 입 귀 모두 너무 새파랗다

눈꼽과 눈썹이, 五月의
풀밭이 되는지
물안개 자욱한 강기슭이 되는지
양털구름 조용히 넘어가던 산마루에도
초록치마폭만 시끄럽게 펄럭거린다
그래 그래, 나이란 확실히 먹는 것이야
먹는 족족 소화되어 없어지는 것이야
세상이 점점 젊어지는 게 분명하고
젊다못해 점점 어려진다는 거야 확실히

POME

유안진
65년 〈현대문학〉등단
시집「달하」「구름의 딸이요 바람의 연인이어라」「다보탑을 줍다」등
시인선「빈 가슴을 채울 한 마디 말」등 12권의 시선집 상재
수상 정지용문학상 소월문학상 특별상 월탄문학상 펜문학상등 수상

Rain's Love

Moon Jeong-hee

I want to pluck the bones out of the body.
I want to be water.
With a fragrance softer than water,
I want to seep in.

I want to wet
The roots of your darkness
To the very end of the thorn.

Being hugged
Within your sleep,
I want to cleanse totally
The things on earth.

I want to open their eyes.

비의 사랑

문 정 희

몸속의 뼈를 뽑아내고 싶다.
물이고 싶다.
물보다도 더 부드러운 향기로
그만 스미고 싶다.

당신의 어둠의 뿌리
가시의 끝의 끝가지
적시고 싶다.

그대 잠 속에
안겨
지상의 것들을
말갛게 씻어 내고 싶다.

눈 틔우고 싶다.

POME

문정희
1969년 《월간문학 》 등단
수상 2010년 제7회 시카다상
경2007~ 고려대학교 문예창작학과 교수
시집 『다산의 처녀』 외 『카르마의 바다』 외 다수

Old Cow

I Geon-cheong

Cow, you cow, old and senile. Will you call me moo? Like a stray star that falls into the fir grove by Naeso Temple in the small hours, like the goosander that has gone to Kangsan-myon or Kangha-myon to dive into the pond in the eco-forest, will you blink your eyes? Will you ring the bells hanging on your neck? Will you call me moo? Cow, you cow, old and senile.

늙은 소

이 건 청

소야, 늙어서 힘없는 소야 음메하고 불러 줄래?. 새벽 한 시나 두 시, 내소사 전나무 숲에 떨어지는 부스러기별처럼, 강상면이나 강하면 생태숲 못 속으로 자맥질하러 간 물닭처럼, 눈이라도 꿈 벅여 줄래? 목에 걸린 워낭이라도 울려 줄래?. 음메하고 불러 줄래?. 소야, 늙어서 힘없는 소야.

POME

이건청
소속 한양대학교 (명예교수)
1967년《한국일보》신춘문예 등단
수상 2010년 제3회 목월문학상
현) 한국시인협회 회장

Marks on the Buttocks

Mun In-su

After bulldozing green hills, an industrial complex has taken its place. The huge chimneys are waving their fists towards the skies as if they were lifting something together. In the hills behind the village where ruin and remote fear are rushing in like thunder.

The mugwort I'm sitting on must be a fragrance that has accumulated forages, a force that has sprouted green over several millennia. Are they an industrial complex of ultimate disobedience or of my mind?Indeed, there are outcries several people produce all at once. The movements of the mugwort are pushing out the traces of my buttocks with babbling noises.

엉덩이 자국

문 인 수

초록 야산들을 깔아뭉개고 공단이 들어섰다. 거대한 굴뚝들은 이제 그 무엇을 일제히 들어 올리나, 하늘에다대고 마구 주먹감자를 먹인다. 폐허가, 먼 공포가 우레처럼 몰려오는 이 뒷동산,

내가 깔고 앉은 쑥들은 도대체 얼마나 오래 쌓인 향기냐, 몇천 년째 계속 새파랗게 돋아나는 힘이냐. 역천逆天의, 내 마음의 일개 공단을 쳐부수는 것일까. 참 여럿이 한꺼번에 내지르는 함성이 있다. 쑥들이, 내 엉덩이 자국을 밀어내는 동작들이 자잘자잘 소란하다.

P O M E

문인수
1985년 〈심상〉등단
시집『뿔』『홰치는 산』『배꼽』외 다수
미당문학상 편운문학상수상

Garden Flower

I Mu-won

A wild flower is still in bloom in that place.
It has not withered over a period of 50 years.
At times I would put my bag or school uniform in pawn
For my meal and drink.
When the poor college student from the countryside dropped in,
She often offered me a meal before I had drinks,
Stealing a look at the owner.
Youngja, at one time or another you shyly offered me
A bottle of local wine to take to my father in the countryside.
Youngja, who watched me pitifully
Under the street lamp shining from the utility pole--
Your pure soul looked so lofty yet vulnerable.
The white wine house that stood
By the stream at the Seongdong Station,
Where the flowing stream has been paved.
Are you still preparing the dinner table to allay my hunger?
But you must have become someone's good mother or good wife.
Just as only love remains if you subtract desire from love,
Sad Youngja remains as dregs of time,
and yet still blooms as a garden flower of tremulous pure love.

들꽃

이 무 원

그 곳엔 아직도 들꽃 한 송이 피어 있다
오십 년이 지난 지금까지 시들지 않는다
가끔 술값으로 가방도 맡기고
교복도 벗어놓고 나오는
초라한 시골 출신 대학생 찾아들면
술 대신 밥 먼저 요기하라고
주섬주섬 주인 눈치 보며 상을 차리던 영자 씨
명절이 되면 백화수복 한 병 사주며
시골 아버님 갖다 드리라며 수줍어 하더니
전봇대 가로등 아래서 애처롭게 나를 바라보던
너무 순한 영혼 다칠까 조심스러웠던 영자 씨
지금은 백화점이 들어선
지금은 흐르던 개울물도 복개된
성동역 냇가에 있던 술집 흰 집
아직도 허기진 나를 위해 상을 차리시는가
그도 이젠 남의 현모양처 되었으리
사랑에 욕망을 빼면 아름다움만 남듯
세월의 앙금으로 남은 슬픈 영자 씨
떨리는 순정의 들꽃으로 아직도 피어 있다

P O M E

이무원
1979년 《詩文學》 등단
시집 『그림자 찾기』 『서하일기』 외 3권
응시동인

Pygmalion' s Bean Pod

I Geon-seon

Hathor' s ecstasy that came into
the first glance, the very first glance
Hakuna-Matata

Happiness' icon detected over and over again
Spero-spera-alegria

Pygmalion' s bean pod that renews and renews
Sweet realization in exhilaration

My wife who came as flower and
became poesy
Karma with P.

* Pygmalion: a character in Greek mythology symbolizing an ultimate wish-fulfillment, who breathed life and personality into his dream ivory sculpture Galatea (meaning "sleeping love"), turning it into a human being and eventually marrying her.
* Hathor: a goddess of love, beauty, and joy, in Egyptian mythology.
* Hakuna matata: "Don' t worry, it' ll be all right."
* Spero spera: "There' ll be hope as long as one is alive," in Latin.
* Karma: person' s acts in one of his successive existences, regarded as deciding his fate in his next existence.
* Alegria: "ecstasy" in Spanish.

콩깍지

이 건 선

첫눈에 맨 첫눈에 쏙들어온 하토르의 황홀
하쿠나 – 마타타

두고 두고 들켜가는 幸福의 아이콘
스페로 – 스페라 – 알레그리아

새록 새록 새로워지는 pygmalion콩깍지
신명속 살맛나는 깨달음

꽃으로 와서 詩가 된 아내
朴福心과의 karma

* Pygmalion : 그리스신화. 꿈을 조각한 상아 조각 작품 갈라디아('잠자는 사랑' 이라는 뜻)에 생명과 인격을 불어 넣어 인간을 만든 뒤 결혼까지 한 지성감천의 상징적 주인공.
* Hathor 하토르 : 이집트신화. 사랑,美 ,기쁨의 女神.
* 하쿠나–마타타 : 아프리카 스와할리어로 '걱정하지마 잘될거야'
* 스페로–스페라 : 라틴어로 '살아있는 한 희망은 있어'
* karma : 業, 因緣.
* 알레그리아 : 스페인어로 '환희'

POME

이건선
1978년 《현대문학》 시 추천완료
1998년 국민훈장 목련장 수상
2007년 허난설헌 시부문본상 수상
시집 『피그말리온 콩깍지』 외 8권

Original Being, Its Lovely Metamorphosis
– Recording Sketch No. 3

Gim Du-hwan

At first, cautiously, barely
Faintly, gently, spreading spreading
As spirit soars and soars
Bloats, gathers, fully
Thickens, becomes dense, overmuch
Savor and its glow
Glow and its force
Force, strange power, lovely metamorphosis
Ahem, Whew, Whoopee
Roams in all quarters, ferrets out
Mixing and then tiding up things
Squirting high and ringing
Reverberating high into the sky
The peace god' s bugle roars
The infinite melodies
Tumble and dance
Calmly, softly, nodding
Shivering, merging loudly.

본유 그 호변虎變

– 녹음 스케치 · 3

김 두 환

처음엔 조심조심 가까스로
여리게 곱게 번지다 번지다
기氣 오르고 오르는 대로
더 불어나다 더부룩이 뭉쳐나다
무장 짙어진 우거진 버거운
풍미 그 빛발
빛발 그 위세
위세 그 호세豪勢 – 호변虎變
어험 휘휘 얼싸
사방을 들랑거리며 들추다가
더 높일까 뻘뻘
뭉켜 대면서 매기단하는 일순
뼘들이로 솟구쳐 울리는
하늘높이 울려 퍼지는
평화신平和神 나팔소리 소리소리
그 무한 가락 출렁출렁 너울너울 다시
잔잔히 사르르 끄덕끄덕
아늘거리다가 툭 툭 암지르는구려.

POME
김두환
시집 『읊는 가락에 영그는 그리움』 『가을비 박람회』 외 5권
시선집 『무지개 머금은 들국화』
제2회 영랑문학상(시), 제 10회 허균문학상(시) 수상
한글문화연구회 이사,

Rice-Bowl

Song Hi-bok

In my native place that has brought me up from my childhood, the rice-bowl sounds like rice-platter. Rice-platter sounds like clatter. In my place where I grew up from early childhood, if someone somehow pronounced rice-platter in a low tone of voice, referring to the rice-bowl which reminded of beloved appetite, it seemed to sound clatter-clatter. Rice-platter, which belonged to my primordial mother-tongue, seems to continue to sound clatter-clatter by containing or vacating the world's most noble things.

Song made his debut as a literary critic in 1990 through the Chosun-Ilbo literary contest. In 1995 his work of film criticism was chosen for a prize by the Sports Seoul newspaper. In 2001 one of his short stories was selected by the Buddhist Newspaper in its literary contest. He is a professor at Jinju Education University, in the Korean language education department.

밥그릇

송 희 복

내 어릴 적부터 자라온 곳에서는 밥그릇을 박거럭이라고 소리를 낸다. 박거럭하고 소리를 내면 마치 달가닥 하는 소리가 나는 것 같다. 내 어릴 적부터 살아온 곳에서는 왠지 모를 그리운 식욕이 묻어나올 것만 같은 밥그릇을 두고 박거럭, 박거럭 하고 이름 나직이 부르면 때로는 달가닥, 달가닥 하는 소리를 비슷이 내는 것 같다. 나의 가장 원초적인 모국어인 박거럭은 이 세상에서 가장 고귀한 것을 담아내거나 비움으로써 달가닥, 달가닥 하는 소릴 끝내 거듭거듭 내는 것 같다.

POME

송희복
1990년《조선일보》신춘문예 평론당선
1995년《스포츠서울》신춘문예 영화평론당선
2001년《불교신문》신춘문예 단편소설당선
현) 진주교육대학교 국어교육과 교수

Love of Mother

Gim Jeong-yun

Trudging through past seasons
You appear dim and discolored.
All your life cuddling your offspring,
You've stayed green like the bamboo leaves
In the backyard;
You've matured in your prayers that have seen
The dawn stars reflected in the prayer water-bowl.
I want to nestle up to you,
Clinging to your skirt fluttering ethereally
Under an old pine tree on a wind-swept hill.
As you depart with your hasty gait,
A cloud, shaped like a mother hugging her child,
Follows in your footsteps.
Mother turning around,
Facing the wind and wave from the pine-tree,
Tipsy with the pine fragrance.
Pray have an eternal rest in peace.
One day I'll come back home to your arms
And fall asleep into your fragrance.

사모

김 정 윤

지난 세월 속에서
걸어오시는 당신은 흐리고
색이 바래 있습니다
자식의 길라잡이로 평생을
뒤란의 댓잎처럼 프르고,
샛별이 정화수에 어리도록
기원하던 염원으로 성장했습니다
솔바람 언덕 노송 아래
우화등선하듯 나풀거리는
당신의 치맛자락을 잡고
나, 어리광 피우고 싶은데
흐릿한 형상으로 종종걸음 떠나시는
뒤를 모자상 닮은 구름이 따릅니다
솔바람 물결소리 품에 안고서
송화향기 그득 취하시며
돌아서는 어머니
천겁을 편히 쉬시옵소서
언젠가 당신의 품으로 돌아가
그 향기에 묻혀 잠들렵니다.

POME
김정윤
2011년《다시올문학》수필등단,
현) 한국엔티에스그룹 회장
저서『믿음의 땅에서 디아스포라 까지』
자서전『삼밭의 쑥』1. 2 권

Subdued Outcry

Gim Gi-san

Nothing in the world is worthless.

People, who are ignorant about the color of grass,
Being drunk with glorious hue and scent,
Call foxtail, barnyard grass, amaranthus, pigweed
And those which put down their roots deeper still,
While being trodden and torn, all alike, just weeds.

The breaths that endured solitude in the frozen earth
Which carries the visible texture of dew and stalks of wind
On the vein of the leaf.

Isn't it the weeds that cover the desolate land?
Are you aware of the subdued outcry of the downtrodden plantain?
Do you know where the last kiss of the twilight end?

낮은 외침

김 기 산

세상에 하찮은 것은 없다

화려한 색상과 향기에 취해
풀빛을 모르는 사람들
강아지풀, 피, 소비름, 명아주,
밟히고 찢겨도 더 깊이 뿌리를 내리는 것들
모두 싸잡아 잡초라 부르는데

언 땅 속에서 적막을 견딘 숨결
잎맥에 이슬의 결이 맺혀 있고
바람 줄기가 들어 있는

저 황량한 땅을 덮는 것
잡초들이 아닌가
밟힌 질경이의 낮은 외침을 아는가
노을의 마지막 입맞춤이 어디서 끝나는지

POME
김기산
월간《문예사조》등단
서울 서문여중 교장 역임, 도서출판 '한터' 대표
시집『노을을 베끼다』
kh4263@hanmail.net

Quince and the Story Afterward

Bak Seung-mi

I continued to write poems about quinces;
My heart sinks
Wherever I meet quinces.

In a quince tree I encountered on my walk
The quinces looked so miserable
As if the wind had made holes in their hearts;
It was painful to leave them there as they were
So I picked them and brought them home in my arms,
Placing them by the sunlit window.
They were just like ten children;
All of them dear as my ten fingers.
I was surprised by my lust for more.

The sight of quinces remind me of my poetry,
they tell me;
These compliments I've cherished as a reward in my career.
While the quinces were dying yellow,
I too, in no time, dyed deeply with autumn.

My ID is mogoa(quince).

모과, 그 이후 이야기

박 승 미

모과에 대한 시를 계속 써 오다 보니
어디서든 모과를 만나면
무너지는 마음이 된다

산책하다가 만난 모과나무에
바람이 숭숭 가슴을 뚫어놓은 듯
모과의 몰골이 말이 아니라
발길이 떨어지질 않아
주섬주섬 따 안고 돌아와서
양지바른 창가에 놓아두고 보니
열 자식이라 많을까 싶고
열 손가락 깨물어 안 아픈 손가락 있을까
내 욕심에 내가 놀랐다

모과를 보면 내 시를 떠 올리게 된다는
말, 말마저도
내 사는 보람으로 느끼며 살다 보니
모과가 노랗게 물이 드는 동안
나도 어느새
가을물이 깊게 들어가고 있었다

내 아이디는 모과(mogoa)다

POME

박승미
1987년《현대시학》등단
문학과 창작 작품상 수상
시집『완전한 포옹』『마음 心』외 2권
mogoa3@hanmir.com

Snow

Hwang Gyeong-sik

Letters sent to the skies

Babbling as on a school trip
Putting dots here and there with stubby pencils

Molding letters with a stirring heart
To conceal a single-track thought
Falling and soaring
Drawing lines like mad

Did the postman of the vacant sky properly deliver
Those numberless words of first love
Pouring down blindly?

눈

황 경 식

하늘로 써 보낸 편지들이다

소풍이라도 나온 듯 재잘거리며
낡은 몽당연필로 마구 點을 찍고

글자를 만들며 두근거리는
외곬 생각을 숨기려
떨어지다가 날아오르고
미친 듯, 금을 긋기도 하는

맹목으로 쏟아지는
저 많은 첫사랑의 말들을
허공의 우체부는 제대로 배달했을까

POME
황경식
경북 의성 출생
1994년 1월《현대시학》등단
시집『실은, 누드가 된 유리컵』
hks99a@naver.com

Fermentation

Jeong Il-geun

Here the snow falls below the snowcap.
Birch trees hide behind the snow one after another,
And we drink tea that has come over the ancient tea route.
It's the Pu-erh tea that is more precious than gold,
Which is quiteabundant here.
Each time the tea arrives, they bury it in the earth, and they
Infuse and drink it once 6 years have elapsed for proper fermentation.
My senior who tells me this story has lived here with his family
For some 20 years.
Just as enough waiting ferments tea, my senior has fermented it
Into fragrance like the scent of good tea, as shown by his
Eyebeams, speech and his personality.
I asked him like what tea I tasted 20 years ago, and
Like what tea I taste now.
He only looked out the window open to the snowcapped hills.
Even though I asked the questions in the manner of a poet,
The fact is I was curious about the price of gold in this country,
The fact is I'm a mammonist who has decayed during fermentation.
He must have already smelt decaying gold.
The snow will fall through the night.
It will not show me anything at all.

발효

정 일 근

여기서 눈은 만년설 아래서부터 내린다
자작나무는 차례차례 눈 뒤에 숨고, 우리는
차마고도茶馬古道 넘어온 차를 마신다
여기서 흔한 금보단 귀하다는 푸얼차[普洱茶] 차란다
차가 올 때마다 땅에 묻었다가, 6년 이상이 지나
적당하게 발효가 되면 우려 마신다는 선배는
이 나라에 가족과 함께 와 산 지 스무 해가 된다
기다리는 세월만이 차를 발효시키듯, 그 사이
선배는 눈빛도 말도 사람도
좋은 차 향기처럼 향기롭게 발효되었다
스무 해 전에 나는 어떤 맛의 차였는지
지금 나는 어떤 맛의 차인지 물었지만
선배는 설산으로 열린 창만 바라본다
나도 안다, 시인인 척 물어 놓곤 내심
이 나라 금값이 얼마인지 궁금한 나는
발효되다 쉬어버린 배금주의拜金主義다
금 썩는 냄새를 선배는 벌써 맡았을 것이다
아마 눈은 밤새 내릴 것이다
나에게 무엇 하나 보여주지 않을 것이다

POME

정일근
1985년 《한국일보》신춘문예 시 당선.
시집 『바다가 보이는 교실』 『기다린 것에 대하여』 등.
소월시문학상, 영랑시문학상, 지훈문학상, 이육사시문학상 등 수상.
경남대 교수. poet@kyungnam.ac.kr

Ebb Tide

Bae Chang-hwan

Children of Dalchang, Seonhak,and Yongam,
hidden in mountain valleys 10 to 20 miles away
from the county center,
go to the middle school in the subcounty.
Children of Suchonri, Seokji, Wonjong in the subcounty
and children of Bongge, Sobawoo,and Waryong
in the vicinity of the town
attend middle school in the town.

Children of Seongsan, Kyongsan, and Yesanri in the town
go out to Taegu city.

썰물

배 창 환

면 소재지서 10리, 20리 산골에 숨은
달창 선학 용암 아이들은 면 소재지 중학교에 오고
면 소재지 수촌리 석지 원정 아이들이나
읍내쪽으로 붙은 봉계 소바우 대바우 와룡 아이들은
읍내 중학교 가고

읍내 성산 경산 에산리 아이들은
대구 나가고

POME

배창환
1955년 경북 성주 출생.
1981년《세계의 문학》작품활동
시집『흔들림에 대한 작은 생각』『겨울 가야산』외 3권
저서『국어시간에 시 읽기』『이 좋은 시 공부』

Evening Prayer

I Eun-bong

It's the evening of another day hastened by all manner of things.
I sit spreading a small mat
Before I go to bed.
I offer prayer gathering up my confused mind.
Like the leaves of age-old gingko trees on Mt. Tientai,
My mind wanes yellow!
In time I'll drop down to the earth.
Then what could bring fear or scare?
It'll be all right if I could enjoy
The trivialthings of another day
Though morning comes again, and
All sorts of pain rush to me.
I hasten to send away the day,
I hasten to hail the day.
What makes today, what makes tomorrow?
I ask again and again
While kneeling before a mirror.
And I offer prayer, scraping and gathering
My mind that crumbles the more the more I ask.
The body only becomes clear
When the mind is clear.

I' m another life.
I offer prayer bowing 100 and then 108 times
If only to fulfill a life, and my share of life.

저녁의 기도

이 은 봉

온갖 일들로 종종댄 또 하루의 저녁이다
미처 잠자리에 들기 전
조그만 방석을 펴고 앉는다
어지럽게 흐트러지는 마음 모아
기도를 올린다 천태산 오래 묵은 은행나무 잎처럼
노랗게 저무는 마음이라니!
때가 되면 나도 땅으로
떨어져 내릴 것이거늘
무엇이 두려울 것인가 무엇이 겁날 것인가
다시 아침이 오고, 아침과 함께 온갖 고통이 밀려올지라도
또 하루의 자잘한 일들
즐길 수 있으면 그만이리라
서둘러 하루를 보내고
서둘러 하루를 맞는 시간
무엇이 오늘을 만들고 무엇이 내일을 만드는가
거울 앞에 무릎을 꿇은 채
묻고 또 묻는다 물을수록 더욱 무너지는
마음 긁어모아 기도를 올린다
마음이 맑아야 몸도 맑을 것 아닌가

나 또한 하나의 생명, 내 몫의 생명을 다하기 위해서라도
백 번, 백팔 번 절하며 기도를 올린다.

POME

이은봉
1984년 《창작과비평》신작시집 『마침내 시인이여』를 통해 등단. 시집으로 『내 몸에는 달이 살고 있다』, 『길은 당나귀를 타고』, 『책바위』, 『첫눈 아침』 등이 있음. 광주대학교 문예창작과 교수, 계간 《시와시》 주간.

At the Buckwheat Jelly House

Jang Seok-nam

What thoughts pass through your mind
while you eat buckwheat jelly?
Expressions at the buckwheat jelly house are lonely.

I think of love while I eat buckwheat jelly
because of the coolness;
the utmost smoothness of flesh;
and the puckery and bitter aftertaste.

And because of the risky handling of the spoon and fork.
Though love is always more cautious than this,
Though love is always more precarious.

I see the glances of one I once loved
even in the buckwheat jelly that slid and broke over the table.
So the expressions in the buckwheat jelly house are all lonesome.

묵집에서

장 석 남

묵을 드시면서 무슨 생각들을 하시는지
묵집의 표정들은 모두 호젓하기만 하구려

나는 묵을 먹으면서 사랑을 생각한다오
서늘함에서
더없는 살의 매끄러움에서
떫고 씁쓸한 뒷맛에서
그리고

아슬아슬한 그 수저질에서
사랑은 늘 이보다 더 조심스럽지만
사랑은 늘 이보다 위태롭지만

상 위에 미끄러져 깨져 버린 묵에서도 그만
지난 어느 사랑의 눈빛을 본다오
묵집의 표정은 그리하여 모두 호젓하기만 하구료

P O M E

장석남
1987년 《경향신문》 신춘문예 당선
김수영문학상 현대문학상 수상
시집 『새떼들에게로의 망명』 외 4권

Starting Sah's Tale*

– Exile's Diary · 5

Gong Goeng-gyu

My boat moors at Baekryun Port
And I enter Noh Island, which was called
Satkat Island in the old days.
I carve wood left from cutting ores, to erect a pillar.
I knead clay and build a roof using oak leaves.
I thus build a three-room grass hut.
I dig a small fountain, I install an oven
to prepare for a living.
Yesterday a young Confucian scholar
brought a stone mortar from the mainland
and put them under the eaves.
He then left by the night ferry.
During the day the monk from the Yongmun temple came,
sporting a long beard, dragging a cane.
He brought a bagful of tea and tea things.
He gazed at the port for awhile
and left along the trail
through the bamboo and camellia groves.
The light reflected from rocks on Mt. Gold
daubed with golden sunlight, beyond the
distant islands, descends with the evening,
lighting lamps in every household of the port.
Boiling tea water brought from the well

amid the honey–suckle,
I start writing a novel,
thinking of Your Majesty.
Though there is no real difference
between the affairs of people, nobles and palaces,
I only hope Your Majesty will open your mind
reading this piece of writing.
Though I' m aware that the novel, disparaged by scholars,
cannot straighten the country' s affairs,
I only hope that this novel will safely arrive in your court.
Since my fate depends upon Your Majesty' s mercy.

* Sah' s Tale is a 17th century Korean classical novel.

〈사씨남정기〉를 시작하며
– 유배일기 · 5

공 광 규

벽련포구에서 배를 대어 옛날엔 삿갓섬이었다는
노도에 들어 노를 깎다 남은 나무로 기둥을 세우고
흙을 바르고 갈잎으로 지붕을 얹어
초옥 세 칸을 마련하였습니다
옹달샘을 파고 솥을 걸어 살림을 대강 갖추었는데
어제는 육지에서 젊은 유림 하나가 확돌을 싣고 와서
처마 아래 내려놓고 밤배로 떠났습니다
낮에는 수염이 한 자나 되는 용문사 스님이 지팡이를 끌고 와
차 한 봉지와 다기를 꺼내 놓고는
대나무 숲과 동백나무 숲으로 난 오솔길을 걸어
포구를 한참이나 바라보다 떠났습니다
먼 섬 너머 햇빛으로 금칠한 금산 바위 빛이
저녁이 되자 포구의 가가호호에 내려와 등잔불을 켭니다
인동덩굴이 지나가는 우물에서 떠온 찻물을 끓이며
폐하를 생각하는 마음으로 소설 한 편을 시작하였습니다
백성의 일이 사대부의 일이 궁중의 일이 어찌 다르겠습니까만
폐하께서 이 글을 보아 마음 열기를 바랄 뿐입니다

선비들이 천시하는 소설 나부랭이가
어찌 나라를 바로잡을 수 있을까마는
나의 운명이 폐하의 눈에 달려있으니
이 소설이 폐하의 안전에 안착하기를 바랄 뿐입니다.

POME
공광규
1986년 《동서문학》 등단.
시집 『말똥 한 덩이』 『소주병』 등
저서 『이야기가 있는 시 창작 수업』 등
한민족작가협회 사무총장. kkkong60@hanmail.net

The Train That Goes to the Mirror

Bak Nam-hui

The train goes to the mirror. That train made up of Indian ink, since billions of year ago, has moved towards the mirror with a growing long tail. The mirror carries a repeat mark, and the train proceeds to the mirror for an endless journey that repeats itself perennially. The moment the train enters the mirror, it becomes a fake, a fantasy train with a repeat mark. Fantasy does not question time, nor the absurdity of the world made up of chains of feed. Hence the train goes to the mirror, it thus becomes Wuroboros. It becomes the rolling metal ring of my childhood, a big moon. Wuroboros lives on its own tail. Chain of feed means eating oneself. The train proceeds. The train runs to eat itself. It races forcefully toward the big mouth that has become a mirror. Inside, Oedipus is crying. Adam too. Ah, but then they are all fakes. Let someone break up this mirror. Ah, that mad...

거울로 가는 기차

박 남 희

기차는 거울로 간다 꼬리에 꼬리를 무는 먹이 연쇄로 이루어진 저 기차는 수억 년 전부터 지금까지 점점 더 긴 꼬리를 달고 거울을 향하여 달려간다 거울은 도돌이표, 영원한 반복의 기나긴 여행을 위해 기차는 거울로 간다 기차가 거울 속으로 들어가는 순간 짝퉁이 된다 도돌이표를 단 환상열차가 된다 환상은 시간을 묻지 않는다 먹이의 연쇄로 이루어진 세상의 부조리를 묻지 않는다 그래서 기차는 거울로 간다 그렇게 기차는 우로보로스가 된다 내 유년시절의 굴렁쇠가 된다 커다란 달이 된다 우로보로스는 제 꼬리를 먹고 산다 먹이의 연쇄는 결국 자기가 자기를 먹는 것, 기차가 간다 스스로를 먹기 위해 기차가 달려간다 거울로 된 커다란 입을 향해 힘차게 달려간다 그 속에서 오이디프스가 울고 있다 아담이 울고 있다, 아, 그런데 저것들은 모두 짝퉁이다 누군가 이 거울을 깨뜨려 다오, 아아, 저 미친,

POME

박남희
1996년 《경인일보》, 1997년 《서울신문》 신춘문예 당선.
시집 『폐차장 근처』, 『이불 속의 쥐』, 『고장 난 아침』, 평론집으로 『존재와 거울의 시학』이 있다. 현재 『시산맥』 주간, 『창작 21』 편집위원으로 있으며, 고려대, 숭실대에 출강하고 있다. nhpk528@hanmail.net

My Name

Bak Jeong-dae

It must have been the soul of a seeker after truth wandering about the snow-capped Himalayas. It must have visited Mongolia's Lake Khubsqul or Kyrgyzstan's Lake Issyk-Koel riding on winds on somesunny days.

On some other days, it may have clung like a tree leaf onto the tail of a trans-Siberia train racing and parting birch forests like hair.

Or else, the librarian of the rooftop library that traversed the white night -- a naive soul that fell asleep near your bright breath, having trippedon the dazzling sunbeams while climbing down the ladder in the morning.

My American Indian name is White Wind's Spirit.

Your name is Wise Hawk Sleeps Every Day.

나의 이름

박 정 대

히말라야 설산을 떠도는 구도자의 영혼이었겠지 가끔 햇살 좋은 날이면 바람을 타고 몽골의 홉스골이나 키르기스스탄의 이식쿨 호수까지 다녀오곤 했겠지

어쩌면 어느 날은 시베리아 횡단열차 뒤꽁무니에 나뭇잎처럼 매달려 자작나무 숲을 가르마처럼 가르며 내달렸는지도 몰라

아니 어쩌면 백야를 횡단하던 다락방 도서관의 사서, 아침이면 사다리를 타고 내려오다 눈부신 햇살에 발을 헛디뎌 그대 환한 숨결 곁으로 골아떨어져 잠들던 철없던 영혼

내 인디언식 이름은 백색 바람의 정령이라네

그대 이름은 지혜로운 매는 매일 잠잔다

POME
박정대
1990년 《문학사상》 등단
시집 『단편들』 『아무르 기타』 외 4권
현재 무가당 담배 클럽 동인, 김달진문학상과 소월시문학상 수상
sugarlessciga@hanmail.net

Glad or Fearful

Pak Mi-ra

My poems I meet in a strange place.

Though I must recognize the poem
that looks at me out of a picture frame
leaning to the left on the wall of
the tea house I visit for the first time.
While my two hands in the pockets
rustle like the leaves of the oak tree,
I cannot open my mouth so readily.

I wipe the frame with the flower-patterned tissue.
I wipe it again pulling my sleeves and
blowing my misty breath.
Underneath the frame there is
the phone number someone has written.
Though there are traces of tear drops
from a broken tea cup,
Luckily it's beside an aquarium that bubbles endlessly;
No one pays much attention to the frame.

It has taken us a thousand years to abandon
eyes and ears.
We can recognize each other
because more than a thousand years have elapsed.

A world where eyes and ears have been erased is
a world where all time has been erased.

There two of us who have become wind
can meet like this,
meet and watch each other,
or quietly dodge shaking.

Struck speechless by the sudden encounter
like a thunder–struck tree,
I get up furtively and come out the door
from the tea house.
The field overgrown with variegated flowers
extends endlessly as if saying,
"A hundred years pass in a jiffy."

반갑거나 무섭거나

박 미 라

낯선 곳에서 만난 내 시 한 편.

처음 가는 찻집 벽에 왼쪽이 기울어진 액자 속에서
나를 바라보는 저 시를
아는 체, 아는 체 해야 할 텐데
주머니 속에 넣은 두 손만 떡갈나무 이파리처럼 부스럭거리며
쉽게 입을 뗄 수 없다

꽃무늬 휴지로 액자를 닦는다
물기 많은 입김을 불어가며 옷소매를 당겨 다시 닦는다
액자 아래쪽에 누군가 적어 둔 전화번호가 있고
찻잔을 들어 탁자를 내려친 듯 눈물방울 같은 흔적도 있지만
끝없이 공기방울을 밀어 올리는 수족관 곁이어서
다행이다 아무도 액자 따위 눈여겨보지 않는다

눈과 귀를 버리는데 천 년이 걸린 우리가
지금 서로를 알아볼 수 있는 건 천 년보다 더 오래 흘러왔기 때문이다
눈과 귀를 지운 세상이란 시간을 모두 지운 뒤에 오는 세상이어서
읽어도 읽어도 끝나지 않는 소설처럼
바람이 된 둘이서만 이렇게 만나지는 것
만나서 물끄러미 바라보거나 흔들림을 조용히 외면하는 것

느닷없는 해후에 벼락 맞은 나무처럼 반쯤 넋이 나간 채
슬며시 일어나 찻집 문을 열고 나서면
그깟 백 년쯤 금방이라고
삐삐꽃 지천인 들판이 끝없이 이어질 것만 같다

POME
박미라
1996년 《대전일보》 신춘문예 시 당선
시집 『붉은 편지가 도착했다』 『안개 부족』 외 1권
수필집 『그리운 것은 곁에 있다』
matarri@hanmail.net

Compression

Ma Gyeong-deok

A walnut cake compresses walnut, A carp cake summarizes carp… The fake supersedes the original. As one forges patterns, an imitation emerges. In the same manner, if one compresses academic history, doctors come out.

A compressed sea exists in the canned mackerel pike; green gingko leaves exist in Gingkomin; Araksil contains constipation. When one compresses crab feet, clothespins appear. The artificial bras contain flat breasts, the wig shrouds a bald head. The flashing girdle compresses the protruding belly. If one repeats compression, some excellent products may emerge.

The seed summarizes the tree, a painkiller summarizes all pain. Likewise, I summarize myself into the three characters of my name. If you unravel the compressed file, so many sentences pour out. There emerges a poor-quality woman who has never been a superior product.

As one omits tedious time with dittos, my husband who puts up with my tedious being, summarizes his boredom with yawns.

압축

마 경 덕

호두과자는 호두를 압축하고 붕어빵은 붕어를 요약하고… 짝퉁은 오리지널을 앞지른다. 무늬를 위조하면 유사품이 나오듯 위조된 학벌을 압축하면 박사도 나온다. 꽁치 통조림에는 압축된 바다가 있고 징코민에는 푸른 은행잎이 있고 아락실은 변비를 담고 게발을 압축하니 빨래집게가 튀어나왔다. 뽕브라는 납작가슴을 담고 가발은 대머리를 담고 짱짱한 거들은 똥배를 압축하였다. 압축을 거듭하면 더러 명품도 나온다 열매가 나무를 요약하고 진통제가 모든 통증을 요약하듯, 나는 이름 석 자로 나를 압축하였다. 압축파일을 풀면 수많은 문장이 쏟아진다. 한 번도 명품이 되지 못한 불량품인 여자가 걸어나온다. 이하동문으로 지루한 시간을 생략하듯 지루한 나를 견디는 남편은 하품으로 지루함을 요약한다.

P O M E

마경덕
전남 여수 출생
2003년《세계일보》신춘문예
시집『신발論』외 1권

Yu Jong-in_I Gi-in_Go Yeong-min

Mun Seong-hae_An Sang-hak_Jo Mal-seon

I Yeong-gwang_Gim ryong_I Seung-hui_Na Jeong-ho

Gu Sun-hui_An Cha-ae_I Hye-mi

Gwon Hyeok-su_Gim Nam-su_Gim Eon

Bak Je-young_Bak Wan-ho_Sim Eon-ju

Go Seong-man_Gwon Mi-ja_Choe Ho-il_Jo Hye-eun

Poems of 100 Major
Contemporary Korean Poets

chapter 02

Yu Jong-in_I Gi-in_Go Yeong-min

Mun Seong-hae_An Sang-hak_Jo Mal-seon

I Yeong-gwang_Gim ryong_I Seung-hui_Na Jeong-ho

Gu Sun-hui_An Cha-ae_I Hye-mi

Gwon Hyeok-su_Gim Nam-su_Gim Eon

Bak Je-yeung_Bak Wan-ho_Sim Eon-ju

Go Seong-man_Gwon Mi-ja_Choe Ho-il_Jo Hye-eun

Fantasy
– Near Wangsang Temple

Yu Jong-in

The king, in the midst of his refuge,
stayed in this secluded place in Paju
like a lotus carved from a chestnut tree.

The cats abandoned in the village
made offerings of their wail
better than eunuchs or court ladies.

In advance of the autumn
the royal carriage left the shade in the hills.

The cats which had left the village
continued to serve the king's shade,
having placed in a royal fashion
the mummy of the grandmother
who had been sent to her grave prematurely.

Dead cats multiplied,
so did their cubs.
Wails faded, wails bloomed.
It was like watching strange flower trees
in the mountain shade.

환幻
– 왕상사 인근

유 종 인

왕은 피난이 깊어서 이 파주 산골에
밤나무로 판 연꽃처럼 머물다 가셨다

마을에서 버려진 고양이들이
내시內侍나 상궁尙宮보다
울음 대접이 극진했다

가을보다 먼저
왕의 어가御駕가 산그늘을 떠나갔다

마을에서 떠나온 고양이들은
그제도
고려장高麗葬 친 할머니의 미라를 옥체玉體처럼 모셔 놓고
왕의 그늘을 섬겼다

죽은 고양이가 속출했고
새끼고양이들도 속출했다
울음이 지고 울음이 피었다
산그늘의, 이상한 꽃나무를 보는 듯했다

POME

유종인
1996년 《문예중앙》 시 신인상. 2002년 《농민신문》 신춘문예 시조당선
2003년 《동아일보》 신춘문예 시조당선
시집 『아껴 먹는 슬픔』 『교우록』 『수수밭 전별기』
산문집 『염전』 『산책』

The Path Where A Slow Song Passes

I Gi-in

A drop of rain falls, melting a hill and a path, digging up a part of the hill and a piece of the path, letting a new path emerge, and making us often lose that path we used to climb down in the old days. Thus people scoop earth in a warm shovel so that a person may not miss a path he is to travel. Today the speech of the bird who has set up a nest at the end of the branch of the mountain path trembles selfishly. Carrying the old man on a flower palanquin in the distance, they climb up a mountain path singing a slow song, dropping a few slow songs and wrapping them with the thick leaves of an oak tree, tying them tightly. And then the short flowers sitting in a pile in the flower shade ask who that old man may be. And a face that has been trodden down and crushed by someone's foot raises its head asking what the hell. And it wants to see clearly again the path where the flower palanquin has breezily passed by.

* Note. 이기인 Lee hade his debut in 2000 through the literary contest held by the Kyung-Hyang Daily. He has published a book of poems Dubious Encyclopedia for Girls.

느린 노래가 지나가는 길

이 기 인

한 방울의 빗방울이 떨어져 산을 녹이고 산길을 녹여서 산의 일부를 파내 길의 일부를 파내 새로운 길이 하나 생겨나게 하여서 예전에 데리고 내려오던 길을 종종 잃어버리게 한다 하여 사람들은 따뜻한 삽으로 흙을 떠서 한 사람이 지나가는 길을 잃어버리지 않도록 한다 그 산길의 가지 끝에 둥지를 올려놓은 새의 말이 오늘은 푸릇푸릇 이기적으로 흔들리고 할 때 저 멀리서 노인을 꽃가마에 태운 이들이 산길을 올라가면서 느린 노래를 부르며 느린 노래를 몇 송이 떨어뜨려 참나무 진한 잎사귀에 싸서 꽁꽁 묶어놓을 때 꽃그늘 아래 수북이 앉아있던 키 작은 꽃들의 물음이 저 할아버지는 누구야 바라보다 누군가의 발바닥에 밟혀서 뭉개버린 얼굴이 다시 이게 뭐야 고개를 들어서 꽃가마 서늘하게 지나가 버린 길바닥을 환하게 다시 보고 싶어 한다

POME

이기인
1967년 인천 출생.
2000년《경향신문》신춘문예
시집『알쏭달쏭 소녀백과사전』

Refusal

Go Yeong-min

Starting to talk at the same time
When the chop sticks touch the same dish on the table
When they encounter each other
As they are about to sit at a vacant seat

Having yielded a chance to speak,
A chop stick or a free seat
I capture your chance to speak,
Your food or your seat.
And, while you stand awkwardly,
I keep seated all through.
How sorry I feel!

As a skinny mother dog fetches food
For her baby and then leaves it alone quietly,
As the dead closes his eyes for awhile,
Forgiving the mourner eating food with his back turned.

After you, after standing there,
Furtively move to another compartment
Of a chance to speak, of a round dinner table, or

Of a clinking subway,

There you find a space a million square meters.

사양

고 영 민

동시에 말문을 열거나
밥상에서 젓가락이 닿은 반찬이 같을 때
빈자리가 생겨 앉으려다가
서로 마주칠 때

겸연쩍게 말문을 물리고 젓가락을 물리고 자리를 물렸다가
떠밀려 내가 먼저 너의 말문을 빼앗고 먹을 것을 빼앗고
자리를 빼앗아
대신 네가 비스듬히 서 있는 동안
내내 앉아 있는 자의
미안함이여!

홀쭉한 어미개가 새끼를 위해
먹이를 물어다놓고 슬쩍 자리를 피해 주듯
등을 돌린 채 밥을 먹는 상주喪主를 위해
망자가 괜찮다,
잠깐 눈을 감아주듯

서 있던 네가 슬그머니
말문의, 둥근 밥상의, 덜컹거리는 전철의
다른 칸으로 자리를 옮긴

내 앞,

백만 평의 자리

POME

고영민
1968년 충남 서산 출생,
중앙대 문예창작학과 졸업,
2002년 《문학사상》등단
시집 『악어』, 『공손한 손』

She, Who is a Fig Tree

Mun Seong-hae

A fig tree still stands by the wall.
She was still getting older along with the wall
While I was standing there
with two children soft as fig tree fruit
after I had taken up the roots and
moved away to a faraway place,
she was still getting older along with the wall.
While I was roaming about the outskirts of the world,
the wall was still her home and center.
When I greeted her with thick knuckles and a hoarse voice,
She coyly pretended to be going somewhere in a hurry.
But it was beneath the wall just a step away,
she had only opened her hands and
stepped down from the wall.

무화과 나무인 그녀

문 성 해

무화과 나무가 아직도 그 담벼락에 서 있네
뿌리를 걷어내고 먼 곳으로 분가를 한 내가
무화과 열매처럼 무른 아이를 둘 거느리고 그 아래 섰을 때도
그녀는 여전히 담벼락과 함께 늙어 가고 있었네
내가 세상의 외곽으로 맴돌고 있을 때도
여전히 담벼락이 고향이고 중심인 그녀
내가 굵어진 손마디와 쉰 목소리로
안부를 묻자 부끄러운 듯
어딘가로 부지런히 가는 척 했으나
그래도 겨우 대일락 말락한 담벼락 밑이었네
손바닥을 벌려 겨우 담장을 조금 내려섰을 뿐이었네

POME

문성해
1963년 경북 문경 출생
영남대학교 국문과 졸업
1998년 《매일신문》 신춘문예 시 당선 2003년 《경향신문》 신춘문예 시 당선
시집 『자라』 『아주 친근한 소용돌이』 외 2권

Mommy

An Sang-hak

Mr. Kwon Jung-sang
Began his life with Mommy and
Closed his eyes with Mommy.
He called Mommy when he could find milk,
He called Mommy when he could not find milk.
The baby hand that waved in the empty sky,
And the last aged hand.

According to an old poet's portrayal,
He was a compassionate life itself.
The joyful love of being able to give milk,
The sad love of being unable to give milk.
All this he must have learned from Mommy.

In that country where Mommy lives,
He must have experienced a reunion
Which could dispense with compassion,
And loud cries must have signaled the rebirth in that world.
Laughter must have been loud.

어매

안 상 학

권정생 선생은
어매로 눈 뜬 삶 어매로 눈 감았다
젖을 찾을 수 있을 때도 어매를 불렀고
젖을 찾을 수 없을 때도 어매를 불렀다
젖내를 찾아
처음 허공을 젓던 조막손, 마지막 늙은 손

어느 노시인의 표현대로라면
선생은 자비로운 삶 그 자체였다
젖을 물릴 수 있어서 기쁜 사랑 慈
젖을 물릴 수 없어서 슬픈 사랑 悲
다 어매에게 배운 것이었을 것이다

어매 사시는 그 나라에서는
더 이상 자비롭지 않아도 좋을 상봉에 겨워
저 세상에 다시 태어난 울음도 컸을 것이다
웃음이었을 것이다

POME
안상학
1962년 경북 안동 출생.
1988년 《중앙일보》 신춘문예 시당선
시집 『그대 무사한가』 『아배 생각』외 2권
artandong@hanmail.net

Congrats!

Jo Mal-seon

I drank decaf coffee
I drank non-alcoholic beer
I' m going through a warless war
I' m having an experience-less experience
I' ve had a sexless sex
I hugged you devoid of you
Will you taste me devoid of me?
May I pay a short visit back home?
I' ll borrow me devoid of me
An institute has newly appeared
At that crossing just there which one can
Experience at an expensive price
Are you worried about obesity?
Eat fat free from fat
Isn' t the first experience too amateurish?
Seriousness is very funny
You say I' m fat
I' m only fat devoid of fat
Look, you too are lifting aloft
You' ve become much lighter
You' ve enjoyed experience devoid of experience
It' s like mink without mink
Don' t get excited about congrats!

Hanging onto a dead wreath
It's time to make an expression devoid of experience.

축!

조 말 선

카페인 없는 커피를 마셨습니다
알콜 없는 맥주를 마셨습니다
전쟁 없는 전쟁을 치르고 있습니다
경험 없는 경험을 하고 있습니다
섹스 없는 섹스를 했습니다
너 없는 너를 안았습니다
나 없는 나를 맛보시겠습니까
저 잠깐 집에 다녀와도 될까요
나 없는 나를 빌려 갈께요
요 앞 사거리에 비싼 값에 경험할
수 있는 학원이 새로 생겼답니다
비만이 걱정 인가요
지방 없는 지방을 드세요
첫 경험은 너무 아마츄어적이잖아요
진지함은 너무 우스워요
내가 뚱뚱하다구요
지방 없는 지방일 뿐인 걸요
보세요, 당신도 둥둥 떠오르잖아요
훨씬 가벼워졌군요
경험 없는 경험을 즐기셨군요
밍크 없는 밍크 같은 것이죠

죽은 꽃다발에 매단 축! 에 흥분하지 말아요
표정 없는 표정을 지을 때입니다

POME

조말선
1998년 《부산일보》 신춘문예 시 당선
《현대시학》 등단
시집 『둥근발작』 외 1권

Half-Moon

I Yeong-gwang

The sky' s eyes
resembling a cooked rice grain
floating over dish water.

The darkness of the universe is rushing
to erase the last eye, the lone last eye.

Having arrived,
it burns all night,
like reinforcements.

* the title of the late Lee Tae-suk' s song.

반달

이 영 광

구정물에 뜬 밥알 같은
하늘의 눈

하나 남은 눈,
반쪽 남은 눈을
마저 지워버리려고

삼천대천세계의 어둠들이 몰려온다

몰려왔는데,
몰려와서는,

온밤 내 활활 태우고만 있다
원군처럼

* 고 이태석의 곡

POME

이영광
1998년《문예중앙》신인문학상
노작문학상 수상
시집「직선 위에서 떨다」외 2권

Technology
– Yes, I sell tears

Gim ryong

Even the monkey drops from the tree, regardless of bottom.
Is that so? I become miserable because of you, who can become nonplussed because of petty things.
I take out the moon full of eyeballs, and I write that tears are red.

An apple drops from an apple tree with a thud.
I become indifferent to you who want to eat bananas.
Whether it' s the monkey that has dropped from the tree, or an apple that the apple tree has let go of, the thrilling tale starts like the old bicycle that has collapsed in the yard of the empty house.

You and I are going through death as if we' re doing something urgent.
That' s so. As if there remain some faces that should have been thrown out of the body, this day descends from the theater more productively than the movie bill-board that has flopped in the box office.

I understand a crack has appeared twinkling in the tears.
It' s a technology sent from the monkey that has fallen from the tree.
It means it will quietly replace the moon hanging in the apple tree that has let go of the apple.

테크놀로지
– 그렇습니다, 눈물을 팝니다

김 륭

원숭이도 나무에서 떨어집니다. 빨간 궁둥이와는 아무 상관없이
그렇습니까? 지극히 사소한 일 앞에서 마음껏 당황할 수 있는 당신을 위해
나는 한사코 불행해집니다. 눈동자 가득 구겨 넣었던
달을 꺼내 눈물은 빨갛다고 씁니다.

툭, 사과나무에서 사과가 굴러 떨어집니다.
바나나가 먹고 싶은 당신으로부터 나는 자꾸 무심해집니다.
나무에서 떨어진 원숭이거나 사과나무가 놓아버린 사과이거나
흥미진진한 이야기는 빈집 마당에 쓰러진 고물자전거처럼 시작됩니다.

당신과 나는 지금 급한 볼일을 보듯 죽음을 지나는 중입니다.
그렇습니다. 몸 바깥으로 던져버려야 할 몇 개의 얼굴이 남았는지
오늘은 언제나 흥행에 실패한 영화간판보다 생산적으로
극장을 내려옵니다.

눈물에 반짝, 금이 갔다고 읽습니다.
나무에서 떨어진 원숭이로부터 테크놀로지입니다.
사과를 떨어뜨린 사과나무로부터 가만히
달을 바꿔놓겠다는 거지요.

POME

김 륭
본명 김영건, 경남 진주 출생, 조선대학교 졸업
1988년 《불교문학》 신인상 2007년 《강원일보》 신춘문예 동시 당선
2007년 《문화일보》 신춘문예 시 당선 2007년 한국문화예술위원회 창작기금 수혜
마산대학교 강사

Season, Rays of Light

I Seung-hui

This day I want to lean on rays of light; I eat a late supper all alone. Opening the refrigerator, I pause briefly while I thrust my hand into the light to bring out a round food container. I whisper to myself, "Those rays of light are all paths." While the evening quietly erases the hills, I eat my meal without uttering a word. When I lean on the light, I become shadow and darkness. This place resembles a room in the water without a bottom to begin with. Yeah, there was such a season once, a season when I dismissed any fear, a winter that etched a long trace of knife over my body when even the moonlight looked scarlet with drops of blood akin to flickering rays of light. The moon has long since passed over the window. The anxiety feels really comfortable while nothing whispers.

The soul bloated with the rays of light wafted through the air all night.
I recall the red and round beams of light on a day when
The moonlight felt cold like ice.
Those rays of light
Flowed down like drops of water
In between the fingers of trees.
The season still sat wearing a heavy overcoat.

I put the remaining food back into the refrigerator and turn on the light. Letters tiny like sesame seeds, tiny letters smaller than seeds of sun plants glow ceaselessly with dull faces. A season has gone away never to return.

시절, 불빛

이 승 희

불빛에 기대고 싶어지는 날, 혼자 늦은 저녁을 먹는다. 냉장고 문을 열고, 불빛 속에 손을 넣어 둥근 반찬통을 꺼내다 말고 저 불빛들, 다 길이다. 중얼거린다. 저녁이 산을 가만히 지우는 동안 나는 아무 소리 없이 밥을 먹었다. 불빛에 기대면 그늘이 된다, 어둠이 된다. 여긴 마치 물속의 방 같아서 애초 바닥 따윈 없는지도 몰라. 그래 그런 시절이 있었지, 두려움 따위는 집어쳤던 시절, 몸에 긴 칼자국을 그리던 겨울. 깜박거리던 불빛 같은 핏방울로 달빛조차 붉어 보이던. 창문으로 달이 지난 지 오래. 아무 것도 소곤거리지 않는 참으로 편안했던 불안.

불빛에 부풀려진 영혼은 밤새 공중을 떠다니고
달빛이 얼음처럼 차가웠던 어느 날 붉고 동그랗던 불빛을 기억한다.
그 불빛들
나무들의 손가락 사이에서
물방울처럼 흘러내렸고
아직도 무거운 외투를 걸치고 앉은 시절

남은 반찬을 냉장고 속에 넣고, 불을 켠다. 깨알 같은 글자들로 가득한, 채송화 꽃씨보다 작고 작은 글자들이 무료한 얼굴로 쉴 새 없이 비춘다. 한 시절이 가서 다시 오지 않았다.

P O M E

이승희
경북 상주 출생,
1997년 《시와 사람》등단, 1999년 《경향신문》 신춘문예 시 당선.
시집 『저녁을 굶은 달을 본 적이 있다』 외 1권
moonpoem@hanmail.net

Camera Diary

Na Jeong-ho

When I hold the camera, I want to take some dictation.
I furtively jot down the autumn day' s trees and birds
I was sorry to see off empty-handed,
the lush faces in my memory which often accosted me, even her name that looked like a leaf that, once gone, would not return.
I clearly note down the lovely stalks of light that called my name and a cut of wailing with those blinding blinking eye-beams there, taking them down with my whole body clicking clicking.
I close up the murky cloud with a sprained ankle sobbing at the edge of the sky, the dusk at the corner that the murky cloud, in passing by limping, erased and squashed, and the star' s glances.
No matter how hard I struggled, I stood in front of a cliff,
so I trembled in fear with wet eyes.
Beyond the clusters of clouds at sunset,
I take the dictation about my father' s life, loading the camera with a new roll of film.

카메라 일기

나 정 호

카메라를 들면 무언가 받아 적고 싶어진다
빈손으로 보내기에 미안했던 가을날의 나무와 새들, 이따금
내게 말 걸어주던 기억 속의 싱싱한 얼굴들, 한 번 가서는
돌아오지 않을 이파리 같은 그녀의 이름도 몰래 적어둔다
짜릿한 순간들을 온 몸으로 찰칵 찰칵 받아 적으며
내게 이름 불러주던 사랑스러운 빛줄기들, 저기 깜빡이는
눈빛들이 부시게 소스라치는 울음 한 컷도 선명하게 받아 적는다
하늘가에 울먹이던 발목 삔 먹구름, 그 먹구름이
절뚝이며 걸어가다가 지우고 뭉개버린 모퉁이의 어스름,
별들의 눈짓도 가까이 당겨본다 아무리 벗어나려고 몸부림쳐도
자꾸만 벼랑 앞이던, 그래서 두려움에 떨리던 어린 날의
촉촉한 눈망울, 그 가녀린 눈망울 너머로 그리운 아버지가
뭉개 뭉개 걸어오시고, 저녁의 뭉개 구름송이 너머로
새 필름을 갈아 끼운 내가 아버지의 한 생을 받아쓰기 한다

POME
나정호
무크지와 사외보 꽁트작가로 활동
문화예술진흥기금 수혜, 신라문학대상, 해양문학상수상
시집 『불안한 꿈』 육필시선 『달콤한 흔적』, 희곡집 『첼로』
napoes@naver.com

Moment

Gu Sun-hui

I do not know how one should unfold it.
Though one may say one grips the bridle firmly
Or else the bridle is loose,
One could have missed the timing
While making clumsy calculations.

One can see before long
That the paths that have followed one another
With persistent epic or lyric qualities,
That they have been erased in an instant
Or are in a dubious state.

Though one wanted to unfold again the past paths
One froze with premature fear.
The brevity of the moment
That persisted with periods or pauses
Only took one gasping breath.

잠시

구 순 희

어떻게 그걸 펼쳐야 하는지 모른다
고삐를 움켜잡았거나 느슨하거나
둘 중의 하나라고 하지만
어설프게 머리 굴리다가
타이밍을 놓쳤겠지

끈질긴 서사나 서정으로
그렇게 이어져 온 길들이
일순 지워져 버렸다는 걸
왠지 썩 미지근하다는 걸
오래 들여다보지 않아도 안다

지나온 길 펼치고 싶다가도
지레 겁먹어 시퍼렇게 얼었다
쉼표, 마침표로 이어지는
순간의 짧은 시간도
숨 한번 훅, 들이쉴 뿐이었다

POME

구순희
경남 양산 출생
1981년 《현대시학》등단
시집 『수탉에게 묻고 싶다』 『내려놓지 마』 외 4권, 한국문협 작가상 수상
시와 미학 편집자문, ballpen9@hanmail.net

Sundry Flowers

An Cha-ae

Azaleas are everywhere over the plain-looking hills
in the early spring.
A flower resembling Cinderella.
A flower rather resembling Kongjui and Shimchong.
Without a fringe leaf on bent and thick stems,
An azalea that has bloomed without a proper calyx.
This abrupt pink was a challenge,
much more than charm or allure;
Not because the flower was pretty.
Not because the petals were plentiful and voluptuous.
Plain-looking hills and haggard trees
enlivened the flower.
The trembling wet eyeballs stuck into the soiled face.
The shining inner flesh was glimpsed
in between old garments.
The princes and governors were helpless
in front of this abrupt beauty.
They were shiftless caught in the Zen question
of a lifetime.
The myth of the azalea' s color will contiue
as long as the new spring comes.

허드레 꽃

안 차 애

허름한 초봄의 산자락에 진달래 지천이다.
신데렐라를 닮은 꽃.
콩쥐와 심청이를 더 많이 닮은 꽃.
휘고 야윈 마른 가지에 주변 이파리 한 장 없이,
변변한 꽃받침 하나 제대로 못 갖추고 핀 진달래!
그 돌연한 분홍빛은 매력도 고혹도 넘어 도발이었다.
꽃이 예뻐서가 아니었다.
꽃잎이 풍성하고 농염해서도 아니었다.
허름한 산과 가난한 나무가 꽃을 한껏 살린 것이다.
때 묻은 얼굴에 박혀있는 떨리는 젖은 눈동자!
낡은 입성 사이로 보이는 부신 속살!
생각도 못한 돌연한 아름다움에
그만 왕자님도 원님도 속수무책이었던 것이다
꼼짝 할 사이도 없이 일생의 話頭에 걸려버린 것이다
새 봄이 오는 한
진달래 빛 신화는 계속 될 것이다.

POME

안차애
97년《월간 열린시》 등단,
2002년《부산일보》신춘문예당선
시집『불꽃나무 한 그루』

Step by Step

I Hye-mi

You go out and
I am absorbed.

This is an erroneous habit
Concerning an old door.

If you wink,
I hurriedly
(Squander).

It is time for the music that was involved with your breathing
To depart shaking its head.
Tomorrows evaporate like bouquets of mist flower
In between yesterday' s fingers and today' s scruff of the neck.

It was gradually dawning on us
(Though we didn' t try to respond)
That they were barely surviving,
Linking beat to rhythm.

Ah, this sad mind doesn' t even have a skill
To double up with laugher.

Our pinks are pressed to death
Under the motor car' s tires.

스텝 바이 스텝

이 혜 미

너는 나가고
나는 흡수된다

이것은 오래된 문에 대한
어긋난 습성이기도 해서

네가 윙크하면
나는 서둘러
(탕진한다)

너의 호흡에 연루되었던 음악들이
고개를 저으며 떠나가는 시간
어제의 손가락과 오늘의 목덜미 사이로
안개꽃 다발처럼 증발하는 내일들

애써 대답하지 않아도, 우리는 그것이
선旋에 율律을 잇대어 간신히 연명하는 것임을
눈치 채고 있었다

아, 이 슬픈 속도
요절하는 기술조차 없어

자동차 바퀴에 압사당하는
우리의 분홍들

POME
이혜미
건국대학교 국어국문학과
2006년 《중앙일보》 신인문학상등단
시집 『보라의 바깥』
panpolove@naver.com

Eden Health Clinic

Gwon Hyeok-su

Ascites gathers up,
keeping the stainless press-cooker always round.
As the perilous time, ready to burst out, contracts,
the darkness deprived of the goat' s cries, is darker than
the market' s lanes.
The jaundiced father gets the phone-call at Eden
and goes out to look for the goat become clay.
With the reins, handed down from generation to generation,
coiling around the neck,
He goes away grasping life' s overdue balance.
No-man' s islands, all hills,
the black goat' s Eden.
He comes back leading a black goat
without liver, gall-bladder or toe-nails,
with bare feet dragging slippers.
Eden, devoid of grass;
the black goat' s cries
contained in a plastic pack
don' t even look back.

에덴건강원

권 혁 수

복수가 차올라
스테인리스 압력솥은 늘 둥글다
터질 듯 위태한 시간이 졸아 들면
염소 울음 사라진 어둠이
시장 골목보다 검다
황달 아버지
에덴으로 걸려온 전화 받고
흙이 된 염소를 찾으러 간다
대물림 한 고삐를 칭칭 목에 감고
치러야할 생生의 잔금을 챙겨들고 간다
언덕뿐인 무인도
흑염소의 에덴
슬리퍼 신은 맨발로
간도 쓸개도 발톱도 없는
흑염소 한 마리 찾아 끌고 온다
매애매애
팩에 담긴 흑염소의 울음소리로
풀 없는 에덴
뒤돌아보지 않고

POME

권혁수
1981년 《강원일보》 신춘문예 소설 당선
계간 『미네르바』 시 등단(2002년)
서울문화재단 2009젊은예술가지원 선정, 현대시작품상 수상
시집 『빵나무아래』 kwon1206@hiramail.net

There's a Path Within the Chest

Gim Nam-su

Who hid it there?
I shove my hand deep in the chest.
A meandering wet path emerges.

An asylum for the aged nicknamed Pleasant House
Where aging people curious about the outside world
Vie one with another for a place by the window.
A warped path in each shoe shelf or a path with torn seams:
They are warm rubbing each other's back.
A dead leaf visits only the shelf of Boksun
Who returns home on someone's back
After roaming through the mire pulling somebody else's path.
The daughter who briefly visited the place the year before last
Has not been heard from for a long time.
Misgivings frequently go out in search of a path
Though one hides deep in the chest
The path one has been carrying just in case.
The lone path that was abandoned gropes along and comes back
And lies down weary, unable to gulp down a mouthful of water.
Though the gathered seniors coax and console,
The addresses folded manifold cannot leave the body,

The names only lingering in their mouth.

The anxious fretting dawn turns around suddenly.

As soon as the pair of arctic boots in the chest snuggles into the arm,

A path that lives only within memory rushes out.

A water way dawns beyond the uvula of the old man suffering from dementia.

장롱 속에 길이 있다

김 남 수

누가 숨겨놓은 길일까
장롱 깊숙이 손을 넣어본다
구불구불 질척한 길 하나 걸어 나온다

바깥세상 궁금한 노인들 창가 자리다툼 잦은
양로원 '즐거운 집'
칸칸 신발장마다 뒤틀린 길, 솔기 터진 길
서로 등 비비며 따뜻하다
가끔 남의 길을 끌고 진창 속 헤메다
업혀 오는 복순씨 칸만 가랑잎 한 장 들락거린다
지지난 해 설핏 다녀간 딸은 소식 끊긴지 오래
신고 온 길 혹시나 싶어 장롱 깊숙이 숨겨도
불안은 수시로 그 길 찾아 나선다
놓고 온 외길 더듬거리다 돌아와
몸져눕는 밤, 물 한 모금 넘어가지 않는다
몰려든 노인들이 어르고 달래도
꼬깃꼬깃 살붙이 주소는 몸속을 빠져나올 줄 모르고
입안에서만 뱅뱅 도는 이름
혀를 끌끌 차던 새벽이 문득, 장롱 속
낡은 털신 한 켤레 가슴에 안기자

기억 속에만 사는 길이 달려 나온다
갸르릉, 치매노인 목젖 너머 물길이 트인다

P O M E

김남수
충남 부여 출생, 본명 김남순
2008년 《평화신문》 신춘문예 시 당선, 2009년 《시안》 등단
2011년 서울문화재단 창작기금수혜
nsk29@hanmail.net

Face

Gim Eon

If you press here, it' ll pop up there
Just as, if you press the keyboard,
Music will spring up.

Over this surface with a large width
The sinking spot and the surging spot
In turn show shifting expressions.

It may be very pleasant today
And tomorrow will sink low.
Can you see the fingers jumping
Over the earth surface collapsing each moment.

We' ve walked with zeal up to this place,
Over the keyboard.

How long shall we stay?
We' ll return after a moment of seeing the sight.

얼굴

김 언

여기를 누르면 저기가 나오겠지요
건반을 누르면 음악이 튀어나오듯이

드넓은 장소를 가진 이 표면에서
함몰되는 지점과 융기하는 지점이
번갈아 가며 표정을 바꿉니다

오늘은 매우 유쾌할지도 모릅니다
내일은 매우 가라앉을 것처럼
시시각각 일그러지는 지표면을
뛰어다니는 손가락이 보이나요

우리는 이곳까지 열심히 걸어 다녔습니다
건반 위에서

얼마나 오래 머무를까요
잠시 경치만 구경하고 돌아옵니다

POME

1998년 《시와사상》 등단.
시집 『숨쉬는 무덤』 『거인』 『소설을 쓰자』
제 9회 미당문학상 수상

Poet Kim Chung-kyu

Bak Je-yeung

While alive he was a mourner-slave.

He said: "If someone relied on my mourning
And could create a tear tiny as a mustard seed
In a sear and dried wasteland of the soul,
I'll mourn on your behalf
Till I become a dark-blue reservoir in the end."

He who was the world's mourner-slave

Has
Finally
Become a reservoir of the world.

시인 김충규

박 제 영

살아서 그는 곡비哭婢였네

내 울음에 기댄 누가 있어
마르고 가문 영혼의 황무지에
겨자씨 같은 눈물 하나 맺힐 수만 있다면
마침내 검푸른 저수지가 될 때까지
당신들을 대신해서 내가 운다던

세상의 곡비였던

그가
마침내
세상의 저수지가 되었네

POME
박제영
강원도 춘천 출생
1992년 《시문학》등단
시집 『뜻밖에』, 『푸르른 소멸-플라스틱 플라워』
〈빈터〉동인, 〈a4〉동인sotong@naver.com

Dawn's Moon

Bak Wan-ho

I saw it on my way to work at dawn.

A man who could not return home all night--

His haggard face
Stayed put,
Stuck between apartment buildings under construction.

The man who was caught red-handed
Doing something ridiculous without a job;
Being unable to go back to his wife
Or to his girlfriend,

He shivered and fretted helplessly
In the month of November by lunar calendar.

새벽달

박 완 호

새벽녘 출근길에 보았다.

밤새 귀가하지 못한
한 사내

파리한 얼굴이
공사 중인 아파트 건물 사이에 끼인 채
옴짝달싹 못하는 걸.

직장까지 잃은 주제에
딴 짓 하다 걸린 남자가
마누라한테도 못 가고
애인한테도 못 가고

하릴없이 떨고 있는
음력 십일월.

POME
박완호
충북 진천 출생. 1991년 《동서문학》 등단.
시집 『아내의 문신』 『물의 낯에 지문을 새기다』 외 2권
'서쪽' 동인 및 시인축구단 '글발' 회원. 김춘수시문학상 수상.
parkwanho@hanmail.net

Tail

Sim Eon-ju

The radishes construct a path before me.
They lay down an asphalt road,
waving their buttocks.

In what haste,
they leave without putting on underlinen.

In the vegetable garden, a late-coming sun
pats a loose bottom, and
pats the clay exhausted
as after child-birth.

The cloud, blowing up cloud,
makes a cotton quilt.

The wood, blowing up wood,
shakes mobile toys.
The radish departs
to give birth to babies devoid of eye or nose.

꽁무니

심 언 주

알타리무들이 내 앞에
길을 놓고 간다
엉덩이 흔들며 아스팔트 길을
내려놓고 간다
얼마나 급했던지
속옷도 못 챙겨 입고 간다

텃밭에는 늦게 나온 해가
헐렁한 구덩이를 쓰다듬고
해산한 듯 곪아떨어진 흙들을 쓰다듬고

구름은 구름을 부풀려 솜이불을 짓는다
나무는 나무를 부풀려 모빌을 흔든다
알타리무들이
무무무무
눈도 코도 없는 아이들을
낳으며 간다

POME

심언주
2004년 《현대시학》 등단
시집 『4월아, 미안하다』

Sister's Photo Collection

Go Seong-man

It rains outside the window.

In a time resembling copper plate prints.

A highway with cherry blossoms, barley growing in black and white; the cosmos smiling all white in an old school; mother and father stand uptight clad in deep blue Korean dress; tall aunt and her husband over there, cousins with dark faces; nephews celebrating the first anniversary; boys dark beneath the nose suppressing laughter; girls blown up like steamed bread in yeast.

They whisper, "They have married; others live a long life in love.

Sisters babble for the first time in a long while.

The only child, I go up the stream alone
following the fish, rake the streams with a stick, in black rubber shoes and short pants; I float the paper boats and prostrate in a corner of the room.

The tears I shed then and there must have dried up.
As if meeting an old love,
I watch heaving a long sigh.

누이의 사진첩

고 성 만

창밖으론 비가 내리는데

동판화 같은 시간 속

벚꽃 핀 신작로 흑백으로 자라는 보리 낡은 학교 하얗게 웃는 코스모스 아버지 어머니는 감색양복 치마저고리 입은 채 부동자세로 서있고 저만치 키 껀정한 고모 고모부 얼굴이 검은 당숙 당숙모 돌잔치하는 조카들 코 밑 거뭇거뭇한 머시매들 즈이끼리 웃음을 참느라 이스트 넣은 찐빵처럼 부푼 가시내들

누구와 누구는 결혼했고 누구와 누구는 평생 못 잊고 산다더라

오랜만에 자매들 모여 자글자글거리는 밤

외아들인 나 혼자 물고기새끼 따라 여울을 거슬러 오르고 쪽대 들고 냇가를 뒤지고 검정 고무신 깡똥한 반바지 차림 종이배를 띄우다가 방구석에 엎드려

그때 흘린 눈물은 하마 말랐으리
옛날 애인 대하듯
휴, 한숨 쉬며 본다

POME

고성만
1998년 《동서문학》등단
시집『슬픔을 사육하다』,『햇살 바이러스』외 2권
kobupoet@hanmail.net

Hollyhocks

Gwon Mi-ja

Yecheon Girls High School is located
on the way to my native place.
The way home coils around the walls of
Yecheon Girls High School.
July 4th.
A heap of red hollyhocks lies by the fence.
They are clean because July's god has
cleansed them with rain water.
I want to pick a handful of hollyhocks
to prepare side dishes for the lunch table for
my nephew who lost his mother as a child,
before he goes to the army.

접시꽃

권 미 자

고향 집 가는 길목에 예천여고가 있다
예천여고 담장을 끼고 돌아가면 고향 집으로 가는 길이다
7월 4일,
담장 곁에 붉은 접시꽃이 수북이 놓여 있다
7월의 신께서 빗물로 씻어 놓아 깨끗하다
몇 개쯤 가져다가
군 입대를 앞둔
어릴 적 엄마 잃은 조카
점심상에 반찬 담아내어 놓고 싶다

POME
권미자
2004년 계간《미네르바》등단
다시올문학 편집위원
minary5@naver.com

Closed Eyes

Choe Ho-il

Closed eyes contain our country's cows and grass fields with drifting clouds and scenes of people parting reluctantly.

In the closed eyes

You cannot see people playing the violin or listening to the piano. You may see wind shaking people devoid of legs. Where a television is on that you cannot watch again – If such a man lived there for a while, he'd have died in essence.

After peeping into the world's barn for a moment, he'd have died for good in a manner which prevents people who died with a kind heart from paying a last tribute.

Only old parsley in the parsley field . How could one consume the colored sky freshly?

There where you can see the picture most clearly.

Who will turn the photosensitive film towards today? Like the conceits of a man with legs broken in many places having fallen from May's cliff – thus into the metaphysical black cornea stitched up by the wind.

감은 눈

최 호 일

감은 눈 속에는 우리나라의 소가 있고 풀밭이 들어 있다 구름아 떠 있을 수 있으며 느리게 이별하는 장면도 방영되고 있다

감은 눈 속에는

바이올린을 켜는 사람들 피아노를 듣는 사람들은 담겨 있지 않고 다리가 없는 사람들의 옷을 흔드는 바람이 보인다 다시 볼 수 없는 텔레비전이 켜 있는 곳 잠시 이런 사람이 살고 있다면 그는 죽었으리라 본질적으로

세상의 헛간을 잠시 들여다 본 이후로 그는 영원히 죽었겠다 다정하게 죽은 사람들이 슬프게 조문할 수 없는 수법으로

어린 미나리 밭에는 어린 미나리 아닌 것 뿐 이렇게 채색 된 하늘은 어떻게 푸르게 삶아 먹나

그림이 가장 잘 보이는 저쪽으로

누가 감광된 필름을 오늘 쪽으로 갖다 대나 오월의 절벽에서 떨어져 다리가 여러 군데 부러진 사람의 생각처럼 바람과 바람이 드나들며 꿰매 놓은 형이상학적 시커먼 망막 속으로

POME

최호일
충남 서천 출생
2009년 《현대시학》등단

To Jiwoo

Jo Hye-eun

In a special class

A little girl, tiny as a fist,
Bit a boy who had hands of her size
At that moment, her teeth sounded pop.

Just before aspecial study

She said yellow was blue.
At that moment, the rootless tongue of her blue rolled up
To her soft palate.

Her mother occasionally visited the mental clinic;
At that time she smiled like a toy
In order to become small, solid and pretty
Like a toy, and not her peers.

One day she thrust the quacking sound that
Had penetrated her whole body
Toward a boy who one day left the marks of his fingers
On the arms of all the boys in the class
And left his voice in his mother' s womb.
She then laughed cynically to me.

In the special class

The girl disappeared one day,
She became smaller and smaller;
Her mother urgedher to stay away from the city,
In order not to lose this young devil any more.

지우에게

조 혜 은

특수학급에서

주먹만큼 작은 아이가
자기만한 주먹을 가진 남자애를 깨물었다
그 때, 그 애의 이에서는 '꼭' 소리가 났다

연구수업을 앞두고

노란색을 파란색이라고 말했다
그 때, 그 애의 파란색은
뿌리 잃은 혀가 연구개까지 말려 올라가 있었고

엄마는 때때로 정신과를 방문했다
그 때, 아이는 인형처럼 웃었다
다른 또래의 아이가 아니라 인형처럼
작고 견고하게 예뻐지기 위해

하루는 반 아이들 모두의 팔뚝에 손톱자국을 남기고는
엄마의 자궁 속에 목소리를 두고 온 한 사내아이에게
온 몸을 관통하고 나온 '꽥' 소리를 질렀다
아이는 나를 보며 씩 웃었다

특수학급에서

어느 날 아이가 사라졌다
아이는 자꾸만 작아졌고
엄마는 도시에서 멀어지길 원했다
더 이상은 이 꼬마 악당을 잃어버리지 않기 위해

POME
조혜은
1982년 출생
2008년《현대시》등단
hem0302@naver.com

Gim Se-yeung_Im Hyeong-sin_Jeong Ho

Gim Si-un_Jang Hye-seung_Jang Sang-gwan_Gwon Gi-man

Jo Yu-ri_Gim Hyeon-sin_Choe Gwan-su

Bak Il man_Jong Ha-hae_Gim Ri-yeong

I Hui-seop_Heo Young-suk_Gim Yeung-chan_Bak Jong-in

Bok Gi-wan_Han Sang-rim_I Won-sik

No Un-mi_Yang Geum-hui_Kim Eun-sook

Gim Nin-cheol_Kim Il-ung

chapter 03

Gim Se-yeung_Im Hyeong-sin_Jeong Ho

Gim Si-un_Jang Hye-seung_Jang Sang-gwan_Gwon Gi-man

Jo Yu-ri_Gim Hyeon-sin_Choe Gwan-su

Bak Il man_Jong Ha-hae_Gim Ri-yeong

I Hui-seop_Heo Young-suk_Gim Yeung-chan_Bak Jong-in

Bok Gi-wan_Han Sang-rim_I Won-sik

No Un-mi_Yang Geum-hui_Kim Eun-sook

Gim Nin-cheol_Kim Il-ung

Self-defense of a Heavy Smoker

Gim Se-yeung

I still smoke cigarettes,
not merely because of nicotine addiction.
I do so
because I want to burn down the larva of memory
that eat into the seahorse' s nest and the temporal lobe,
causing headaches.

The ashes of the larva gather in the lung blister,
causing me to pant for breath
like mullets in Sihwa Lake.
The reason I still dote on cigarettes
is I' m an adult-child longing for mother' s tits.

Ruminating the memories of mother' s milk
while I was licking the pestils with my bill
in the oral season in the nest,
retracing the memories of the first kiss
that planted fire flames in my mouth
during the five-senses season when I was
casting my skin.

Like a potter that builds fire in the kiln
breathlessly with old bellows,
I'll breathe deep into my chest and
blow out all my life to the dregs
in order to call in the spirit to fill the last jar.

애연가의 변

김 세 영

아직도 담배를 피우는 것은
니코틴 중독 때문이 아니다
해마의 둥지, 측두엽을 갉아먹고
두통을 일으키는 기억의 유충들을
태워버리고 싶기 때문이다

허파꽈리 속에
유충의 잿가루가 쌓여
시화호의 숭어처럼 숨차하면서도
담배를 빨고 있는 것은
어머니 젖꼭지가 그리운
어른아이이기 때문이다

둥지 속 구강시절
부리로 꽃술을 빨아먹던
모유의 기억을 되새김질하며
허물벗기 하던 오감시절
입술 속에 불꽃을 꽂아 주었던
첫 키스의 기억을 더듬으며

낡은 풀무로 숨 가쁘게
가마에 불 지피는 도공처럼
마지막 항아리에 채울
혼령을 불러들이기 위해
가슴깊이 들이마셨다가
목숨 한 톨 남김없이 불어 내어
풍선으로 띄울 것이다.

POME
김세영
2007년 《미네르바》 등단
*시집 『강물은 속으로 흐른다』외 2권
mokjoin@hanmail.net

Nectar Hermitage

Im Hyeong-sin

I found a fountain hidden at the foot of Nectar Hermitage
Past Medicinal Fountain Temple.
I stayed there for a season drinking that water.
I watch birds while drinking water
I watch flowers while drinking water
I watch the water bottle while drinking water
Passing birds drink water
Asters come down to drink water
Green snakes come over to drink water
By the hedge the tall pea tree drinks water
Shedding yellow petals before they go away
Bhaisajya-guru drinks that water and pats my aching eyebrow
Crape myrtle drinks that water and is all smiles.

Back at Nectar Hermitage
There is not anything
There is no water
There is no fountain
There is no nectar
There is no aster
There is no mountain bird
There is no Bhaisajya-guru
There is no grass snake.

Yes, there are:
The small yard with a rock spring has grown larger
There stands a stone Buddha devoid of any expressions
There stands one big sanctum.

There is one big Buddha
There is one large temple
Several shoes have appeared there
Where there were none in the main building,
Which was not there in the first place.

There is no rock spring that drank water and the drank the sky
There is no medicinal fountain in Medicinal Fountain Temple
There is no nectar in Nectar Hermitage.

감로암甘露庵

임 형 신

물 찾아다니다
약천사藥泉寺 지나 감로암 기슭 숨어 있는 샘 하나 찾아내다
그 물 마시며 한 철 머물렀다
물 마시다 새 본다 물 마시다 꽃 본다 물 마시다 물병자리 본다
지나던 새 물 마시고 과꽃 내려와 물 마시고 초록뱀 건너와 물 마신다
울타리가에 키 큰 골담초 노란 꽃잎 흘리며 물 마시다 간다
약사여래 그 물 마시고 아픈 이마 짚어준다
배롱나무 그 물 마시고 벙싯 벙싯 웃고 있다

다시 감로암이다
없다, 물 없다 샘 없다 감로 없다
과꽃 없다 멧새 없다 약사여래 없다 초록뱀 없다

있다, 돌샘 있던 작은 마당 넓은 마당 되어 표정 없는 석불 하나 서 있다 큰 법당 하나 있다 큰 부처님 하나 있다 큰 절 하나 있다 없던 대웅전에 없던 신발 여럿 있다

물 마시다 하늘 마시던
돌샘 없다, 약천암에 약천이 없다
감로암에 감로가 없다

POME
임형신
전북 정읍 출생
2008년 《불교문예》등단
yim 924@Hanmail.net

Carpenter Bee Bus

Jeong Ho

I get on a vacant bus one stop from the starting point.
As I take a rear seat, a carpenter bee -- since when?-- is flapping its wings around a sweat-smelling seat handle.
The autumn wind prompted him to jump on a journey.
An empty can, thrown underneath a seat asleep at the terminal in a mountain village--
Could its warm breath have seduced him?
Like my life that somehow had a free ride,
the sudden halt made me lose my grip on the handle,
lodging me plump onto the seat.
A pail of my dream was sweet like a honeymoon,
but the empty can was none other than my desperate self.
I quietly grasp myself.
I, still lingering around a hill-top village for decades,
am none other than that carpenter bee.
I finally regain hold of my weary self.
I open the window and let it fly toward the Anyang river.
My head, whose speedometer is out of order, is full of the scent of a pumpkin flower.
Now the winter is a few years away.
My back feels itchy like sprouting wings
as I size up the wax-sealed pension.

호박벌 버스

정　호

시발역에서 한 정류장, 훌빈한 버스에 오른다
뒷좌석에 자리를 잡는데
언제부터 올라탔는지 호박벌 한 마리
땀내 밴 좌석손잡이를 쥐락펴락하고 있다
가을바람에 훌쩍 여행이라도 떠나고 싶었던 걸까
산동네 종점에서 낮잠 자던 버스 의자 밑
나동그라진 빈 캔 단내에라도 꾀였는가
어쩌다 무임승차하게 된 내 삶의 이력처럼
안간힘쓰다 급정차하자 손잡이도 놓치고
털썩 떨어져 시트에 앉지만 좌불안석이다
내 꿈 한 통도 밀월처럼 달콤했지만
이순에 돌아보는 빈 깡통은 나였다
수십 년을 여태 산동네 근처서만 맴도는
내가 한 마리 호박벌이다 기진맥진한 나를
살며시 움켜쥔다
창을 열고 안양천으로 날려보낸다
타코미터마저 고장난 내 머릿속
온통 호박꽃내뿐이다
이제 겨울도 몇 년 앞,
밀랍蜜蠟한 연금年金을 가늠해 보는
내 등이 날개 돋을 듯 가렵다

POME
정 호
2004《문학 · 선》등단.
탈시 동인. 다층사람들 편집동인.
시집『비닐꽃』
jkloppo@unitel.co.kr

Near Dry Grass

Gim Si-un

Chestnuts have dropped over paths worn by time
And now lie in the bush.
Felled by insects or wind,
The baby chestnuts are shedding tears.
Grope for the old paths waiting,
Hidden in the bush eroded by time.
If you want to see someone, go to that place.
When you are tearful, go to that place.
Set out to find old paths hidden
In the hills behind your home village,
Which greets you always with open arms.
There where they welcome you
Over the narrow paths through the forest
Where dry grass waves hands,
You'll see the wind's shadow
Over the paths where insects crawl.
Under the chestnut tree where chestnuts emerge
Briers and brambles are hushed.
The dry grass will wipe your tears resembling dew drops over grass.

마른 풀들 가까이서

김 시 운

세월 지워진 길 위에 밤송이 떨어져
풀숲에 누워 있다
벌레 먹어 떨어진 것인가
바람에 떨어진 것인가
풋밤송이 눈물을 흘리고 있다
시간 깎여 간 수풀 속에 숨어서
기다리고 있는 옛길을 더듬어 보라
누군가 보고 싶으면 그 곳에 가 보라
눈물이 고이거든 그 곳에 가라
언제 찾아와도 가슴을 열고 맞아 주는
고향 뒷산 숨은 옛길을 찾아 나서라
너보다도 더 널 반가워하는 거기엔
마른 풀잎들 손을 흔드는 그 작은 숲길엔
껍질 벗는 벌레들 기어가는 길 위로
바람의 그림자를 본다
알밤 얼굴 내미는 밤나무 아래
들가시와 찔레도 숨을 죽이는 거기
풀이슬 같은 너의 눈물 닦아 줄 거야
마른 풀들 우산을 쓰고서

POME

김시운
충북 보은 출생, 2000 《시현실》 등단
전국 공무원문예대전 행정자치부장관수상, 2007년 모던포엠 본상 수상
제5회 세종문화예술대상 (시부문)수상, 시집 『바람에게 물어나 보게』 외 3권
river49@hanmail.net

River of No Return

Jang Hye-seung

The bubbles that fall together at the Bow Falls--
Just dazzling, as if ten-thousand-year old legends
melted and blended in.
They're all emerald in color.
The water assumesmysterious colors
As if the sky's jade-colored milk spread out--
It meanders with dignity through the rocks.
The rocky hill looks down silently, carrying
tall hills and cliffs on its head.
They say the color of longing has that hue.
The wind shoves the trees towards a perilous place.
The green corps submits to the commands.
The water that cannot return leaves the river of no return
And flows towards an unknown destination.
And Marilyn Munro, who cannot own anything in the end
Is washing the bare head of the rock.
Those who live in the word "love" become
colder as they approach nearer.
The huge hills and cliffs that live watching
Only the chastity of that hue of the water
huddle together.
Remember only me who want to return by all means.
Goodbye.

돌아오지 않는 강
-River Of No Return

장 혜 승

보우폭포에서 함께 추락하는 포말들
눈부셔라, 만 년 전 전설들이 녹아내려 섞였나
에메랄드빛이라네
비취색에 하늘의 젖을 짜서 풀어놓은 듯
저 신비한 색깔의 물
바위들의 가랑이를 빠져 유유히 굽이친다
기암절벽을 머리에 이고 묵묵히 내려다보고 있는 저 바위산
제 무게를 버린 목화송이구름들로
수치스러운 곳을 치장하고 쓰러질 듯 서서
그리움의 속살이 저런 빛깔이다 한다
바람은 나무들을 위험한 곳으로 밀어붙이고
그 명령에 굴복하는 저 짙푸른 군단들
돌아올 수 없는 물들은 돌아오지 않는 강을 떠나
알지 못하는 곳으로 흐르고
끝내 아무것도 가질 수 없는 마린먼로가
바위의 대머리를 감겨 주고 있다
사랑이란 말 속에 사는 것들은 가까워질수록 더 차갑다
저 물빛의 정절만 보고 살아가는 웅장한 기암절벽들도
오들오들 떨며 붙어 있다꼭 돌아오고 싶은 나만 기억해 줘
안녕히

POME
장혜승
경북 의성 출생
2003년 《현대시학》 등단
시집 『씨앗』
hsjang2625@hanmail.net

Banishment

Jang Sang-gwan

Writing an equation of owning versus not owning,
And doing a binomial theorem, nothing remains.
An enigma that doesn't get solved till one's last breath.
That body is settled neatly.
Discarding brand-new clothes and shoes,
Only carrying a backpack,
I've come to the place of my banishment.
My only load is newspapers, all rolled up.
A man who roamed among the stars, lost among
his confused thoughts.
I now spread the newspaper and lay down my body,
Reexamine and recalculate the problems solved in shadows.
I spread equal signs over compressed steps
And desperately haul up the dreams, now receding far away.
As I prop up the sky with my hands,
I realize the earth, the body and the sky come to the same thing.
But my brain cannot adapt to the violent equation.
Hitting the sign in the toilet
I become a snarling locomotive
And let out the steam through my nose.
Warming up the cold air with liquor mixed with wind,
I scribble my memorandum over the final station's floor.

The cluttered prison pulled by gravity –
Why am I unable to escape from it?
Turning around inertly and crouching,
I finally put a question mark.

유배

장 상 관

소유와 무소유 등식을 써놓고
이항정리 하다보면 아무것도 남지 않는다
쉽다 하지만 숨 놓는 순간까지 채득하지 못하는 난제
저 몸은 깔끔하게 풀려 있다
배낭 달랑 둘러메고
한 번 입지도 않은 옷가지며 신발들
줄이고 줄여 유배 왔다
짐이라곤 둘둘 뭉친 신문지뿐
별자리 배회하며 머릿속 정리에 골몰하던 사내
신문지 펴 몸뚱이 누이고
그림자로 풀린 문제 되짚어 자꾸 검산한다
압축해둔 발길 등호로 펼쳐놓고
까마득 멀어져간 꿈까지 사력을 다해 걷는다
두 손으로 하늘 떠받치고 서 보면
땅과 몸과 하늘이 같음도 알겠다 그러나
폭력적인 공식에 도무지 적응 안 되는 머릿속
화장실 표지판 들이받으며
크르릉 기관차가 되어 콧김 내뿜는다
바람 타 마신 술에 한기 데우며 중얼중얼
종착역 바닥에 비망록 쓴다

중력이 잡아끄는 거추장스런 감옥
왜 탈출하지 못하나
끄응 무겁게 돌아 웅츠려 물음표 찍는다

POME
장상관
경남 창녕 출생
2008 《문학.선》 등단
영남시동인
every-wave@hanmail.net

Sorae Estuary

Gwon Gi-man

As I reach Sorae Estuary where sounds moor as songs,
I find the sounds of salt, conches, and crab shears teasing the silt,
Which arrived there before me.
Mounting the wave's refrains
Clams befriend the waves.
Seashells put bowls of salt into their mouth.
Inviting one to travel to Sorae Estuary
Means inviting one to cast anchor into folk songs
And stay there for a few days.
It also means to match the concluding phrases of folksongs
With flooding tide and ebb tide.
Inviting one to Sorae Estuary
Indicates one's wish to rub cheeks at sunset,
To own a salt farm and
To haul up a bucket of unspoiled sounds like Chunil salt.
Saying one has been to Sorae Estuary
means one has been an estuary anchored with sounds
means one has swallowed the sea's words with a seashell mouth
means one has been a lost ship for a few days,
washing a basket of flickering waves with the white salt's mane,
with the wave's scales ceaselessly glittering.

소래포구

권 기 만

소리가 노래로 정박하는 소래포구에 가면
소금의 소리 소라고둥의 소리
콩게의 집게발이 펄 옆구리 간질이는 소리
먼저 와 닻을 내리고 있다
파도의 후렴구를 하나씩 물고
바지락이 파도와 화음을 맞춘다고
꼬막의 입속에 한 됫박 소금을 퍼담는다
소래포구 가자는 말은
소리에 닻을 내리고 한 사나흘 정박해 있자는 말이다
밀물 썰물로 소리의 결구를 맞추자는 말이다
소래포구 가자고 하면
낙조에 볼 비벼 보고 싶다는 말이다
염전 한 채 들여 놓고 싶다는 말이다
상하지 않는 천일염 같은 소리만 한 됫박
꾸덕하게 담아보자는 말이다
소래포구 갔었다는 말은
소리로 정박한 포구가 되어 봤다는 말이다
꼬막의 입으로 바닷말 삼켜 봤다는 말이다
허연 소금의 갈기로 나부끼는 파도 한 소쿠리
무진장 반짝이는 물비늘로 싣고
한 사나흘 멍텅구리배가 되어 봤다는 말이다

POME

권기만
경북 봉화 출생
2006년 월간《문학저널》등단
월명문학상 수상

Dolmen Dinner Table

Jo Yu-ri

2500 years ago, the dinner table must have been heavy. They say there were dinner tables weighing up to 300 tons. Many a time rice bowls fell to death unless the table legs were propped solidly. Folding and unfolding the tables at each meal time was painful. The seniors of the family called the family members to tribal conferences. The informed women of the inner and outer villages, raising the tails of their eyes, egged the men. When young stout men with their trousers rolled up came in packs, their ancestors were cheerful expecting ritual tables loaded abundantly.

Workers, with only stone lances and axes as their tools, bent their spines to serve as props, and, joining their breaths together through fist-sized stones, gathered and rolled the rocks for thousands of years. Preparing full dinner tables for their descendants, stretching their legs under the table, they eased into comfortable slumber. The ill-bread children clashed their swords in front of the ancestral tablets vying with each other to preempt tiny meal tables. Some grandchildren invaded the inner chambers where they were fast asleep with bulldozers and played puzzles using their grandfather' s bones.

The ancestors must be having cracking headaches. The earth' s lids must be opening and closing.

고인돌 밥상

조 유 리

이천오백 년 전 밥상은 무거웠겠다. 삼백 톤이나 되는 밥상도 있었다 하니, 상다리 튼튼하게 괴지 않으면 밥그릇이 상 밑으로 추락사하는 일도 많았겠다. 끼니마다 상을 접고 펴는 일이 여간 수고로운 게 아닐 거라며 가문의 큰 어르신 식솔들 불러 앉혀 놓고 부족회의 열었을 것이다. 소문 접한 안마을 바깥마을 아낙들 눈꼬리 치뜨며 사내들 부추겼을 것이고 정강이 걷어붙인 장정들 떼로 몰려오자 젯상 푸짐하게 받아 잡수실 조상들도 신이 나셨겠다.

연장이라고는 돌창과 돌도끼가 전부인 인부들. 척추 구부려 굄돌을 삼고 맨주먹만한 돌멩이에 서로의 숨구멍을 잇대어 수천 년 동안 뭉치고 굴렸을 것이다. 후손들 위해 거하게 한 상 차려 놓고 상다리 아래 두 다리 뻗고 편안히 잠드셨을 것인데,

조상들에게 이천 오백 그릇이나 밥을 얻어먹었으면서도 개다리소반 차지하기 위해 부모 빈소 앞에서 칼부림하는 후레자식 놈들, 곤히 주무시는 안채까지 불도저를 밀고 쳐들어 와 할배 엉치뼈로 퍼즐 맞추기 하는 손주 놈들 있으니

조상님들 머리꼭지 지글지글 끓겠다, 지구의 뚜껑이 열렸다 닫혔다 하는 것이겠다.

POME

조유리
2008년 계간《문학 선》등단
garam0901@hanmail.net

I Remember the Angle of the Smile

– After watching Don't Cry Tons.

Gim Hyeon-sin

He could not fly away because no one could give him wings.

In a corner of the earth a beech tree, in the picture a man laughing brightly – he begins the daily routine meeting the red star and shadow. The dark desert's knees are shining though they have lost their course.

He wept because he could not bear the life's firy blossoms and the promise he could not erase. So many things he bears on his wings. The shadow of his "Meditation"(1) he tried to vacate is deepening. The brass band, the moist senses, the embraces, are only pictures on that side of the earth.

Standing like a tree, he must have smiled that white smile for the last time; I recall the angle of that smile. They wept by the dark huts (the Dinka people wept.) I also become the desolate horizon like the lost tints of water.

The dark desert cascades like a water-fall.

미소의 각도를 기억하다
– '울지마 톤즈'를 보고

김 현 신

날개를 달아주지 못해서 그가 날아가지 못했다 지구의 모퉁이엔 한그루 자작나무가, 사진 속엔 환하게 웃고 있는 한 남자가, 붉은 별과 그림자를 만나 일상을 시작한다 잠시 방향을 잃은 검은 사막의 무릎이 빛나고 있다

불꽃 인생이, 지우지 못한 약속이 버거워 울었다 그가 날개에 달고 있는, 너무 많은 것들, 비워내려는 '묵상'의 음영이 짙어만 간다 브라스밴드가, 물기 젖은 관능이, 포옹이, 지구 저편의 그림일 뿐이다

한그루 나무로 서있는 그가, 마지막으로 두드렸을 백지 같은 미소, 그 미소의 각도를 나는 기억한다 불빛 없는 움막 따라 (딩카족이 울었다) 울었다, 길 잃은 물빛처럼 나도 쓸쓸한 지평선이 된다 검은 사막이 폭포처럼 쏟아진다

POME

김현신
2005년 계간《시현실》등단
시집『나비의 심장은 붉다』
khs22740@hanmail.net

Eulogy to Shrimps

Choe Gwan-su

A sea, blue and wide
A humble mind cognizant of its own meagerness
With a bent back and
A timid gait.

Longevity with long beards
Rich group dance

Gleaming eyes of wisdom
A vibrant soaring
A mysterious leap-up
Climbing up to the surface.

새우 예찬

최 관 수

푸르고 넓은 바다에서
미미한 존재임을 인정하는 겸양지심謙讓之心
늘 등을 굽히고
조심스런 까치걸음

긴 수염으로 무병장수
풍요로운 군무

튀어나와 반짝이는 혜안慧眼
팔딱이며 쳐 올라가는 역동성

수면으로 뛰어오르는
신비로운 도약

POME
최관수
월간 《문예사조》 등단
시집 『귀향하는 새』 외 4권

Empty Jar

Bak Il man

By the garden overgrown with weeds
A body basking in the sunlight is
pushing the midday at snail pace.
In between creaking knots of bone
The erratic wind shuttles constantly.
The jar that has emptied soy cause, bean sauce
and bits of charcoal
Is drawing a slow trajectory over the yard.
Having sent out all the eggs it had harbored,
the discolored jar rings hollow.
Even flowers that bloomed each month have wilted
long since.
has been deprived of
all laughter.
Mother has put on more weight
maybe because of her changing height.
She has tended the old coughing fits,
having vacated all taste of sweet, salt and hot.
This world she has vacated
has a deepening bottom.
In the empty jar taller than the weeds
Mother takes care of her daily routine.

빈 항아리

박 일 만

잡초 웃자란 마당가에
오도카니 햇살 받는 몸통 하나
달팽이 걸음으로 한낮을 밀고 있다
삐걱대는 뼈마디 사이로
눈치 없는 바람 무시로 드나드는데
간장, 된장, 숯덩이 비워낸 항아리
마당에 천천히 궤적을 긋고 있다
품었던 알들 모두 대처로 내보내고
텅텅 울리는 빛바랜 항아리
다달이 피던 꽃도 시든지 오래다
웃음조차 말라버린 붉은 꽃시절
허리와 키가 점점 같아져서 인지
더욱 둥글어지신 어머니
오래 된 기침도 삭혀내시고
단맛, 짠맛, 매운맛 다 비워내셨다
비우고도 남음이 있으신지
이승의 바닥 더욱 깊어지신다
잡초보다 키 작은 빈 항아리 속에
등허리 돌돌 말린
어머니 들어 계신다

P O M E
박일만
전북 장수 출생
중앙대 예술대학원 문예창작과정(詩) 수료
2005년 《현대시》 등단
시집 『사람의 무늬』 zaca@gg.go.kr

In Ubok Valley

Jong Ha-hae

That illustrious place where stars rolled is charred.
The wind that has come from Mt. Hyung sprays over the earth's skin.
The shoulders of the fallen hill figure lucid in a new terrain.

The youth carried on the shoulder is evident,
but the memory is inscribed wrongfully.

The backs of the grass huts have broken, leaving old bits of bones.
Many words must have been plucked out.

That which still toothes my flesh.

The grass which came out hurt, asks about my wellbeing.
Myriad skies were born without crying, bearing dark eyebrows.
That which becomes red for moments and then goes away
must make statements aimed at me alone.

I who was under his guidance,
I who now have nobody to meet but
say a valedictory to things to part with...
How could I...?

우복골에서

정 하 해

별이 나뒹굴었던 저 역력한 자리, 가맣게 탔다
형산에서 온 바람이 흙들의 껍질을 잠시 잠깐 흩뿌리는 사이로, 무너진 산의
어깨가 새로운 지형처럼 나있어

짐진 청춘은 또렷하나 기억은 틀리게 표기된다

거기 초막의 등들은, 부러져 헌 잔뼈뿐이다
많은 말들이 뽑혀져 나갔겠다

지금껏 내 살을 물고 있는, 것

이미 상해서 나온 풀이, 내 안위를 묻는다 울음 없이 태어나 이마가 검은
하늘이 수만 송이 그렁하게
잠깐씩 붉어지다 가는 그것은, 나에게만 전하는 어떤 진술일 것이다

이제 만날 누구도 없는, 이별해간 것들과 마지막 불을 질러 놓고 돌아서는
그의 슬하였던 나는 차마

POME
정하해
포항출생,
2003년 《시안》 등단,
시집 『살꽃이 피다』 『깜빡』
acusu@hanmail.net

Orion

Gim Ri-yeong

A star resembling me has streaked over the highway.

I cannot catch the star which has gone to Khios Island.

I drew it in the sketchbook with a 4B pencil,

Hugging, binding and pressing it.

The starlight has oozed out, now hanging
Between the eye-lid and the eye-lash.
As I scratched the scales of the paper star
Hot dead branches fell off panting.

The tireless star
like the half-transparent onion skin
strives not to be torn,
drooping over my eyes.

I may be a foolish queen
living far away, believing that
Melope' s face, hardly visible,
hangs at the edge of the eyelash.

Powdered clay begins to fall from the eyes.

Do you ever want to see me?

오리온

김 리 영

나를 닮은 별 하나가 고속도로 옆을 지나갔다

키오스 섬으로 가버린 그 별 잡을 수 없어

스케치북에 4B연필로 그려, 감싸고 묶어 눌러 놓았더니

별빛은 새어나와 눈꺼풀과 속눈썹 사이에 걸려있다.

종이별의 비늘을 긁자
뜨거운 삭정이가 떨어져
숨이 가빠진다.

지치지 않은 별이
반투명한 양파껍질처럼
찢어지지 않으려 애쓰며
내 눈에 달려있는 지

내가 어리석게도, 먼 곳에 사는 왕녀,
한 치도 안 보이는 메로페의 얼굴이
눈썹 끝에 달렸다 믿고 사는 건지

눈에서 흙가루가 떨어지기 시작한다.

너도 내가 보고 싶은 적 있니?

POME
김리영
세종 대학 무용교육과 졸업
Southern Oregon University에서 Art수학
1991년 《現代文學》등단.
시집『바람은 혼자 가네』『푸른 콩 한 줌』외 2권

Bamboo

I Hui-seop

While I listened to you,
my ears have grown by more than 10 meters.

Behind my lips of silence that appeared calm
the huge origin enters into the labyrinth
in search of confidential talk.

How deep a language does it want to haul up
to be speaking no words at all?

Your sentence falls as rain,
you pierce my heart like bamboo shoots.

The whole body becomes roots.
The language' s shade that darkness has groomed
now approaches through the wall named "I."

The month of August flies away carrying your words
through the skies startled into a deep blue.
Each time the wind blows,
the warped words fall.

The vertical words that have passed the silencer
ache severely.

모죽毛竹

이 희 섭

너를 듣는 내내
귀가 수십 미터나 자랐다

평온해 보이는 침묵의 입술 뒤에서
밀어를 찾아 미로 속으로 들어가는
거대한 근원

얼마나 깊은 언어를 길어 올리려고
아무 말 하지 않는가

너의 문장 비가 되어 내리고
내 심장을 관통한 너는 우후죽순

온 몸 뿌리가 되었다가
'나' 라는 벽을 뚫고 온전히 다가서는,
어둠이 길러낸 말의 그늘

새파랗게 질린 하늘 위로
너의 말을 물고 날아가는 8월
바람이 불 때마다 휘어진 단어들이 떨어지고

묵음기를 지나온 수직의 말들이
완벽하게 아프다

POME
이희섭
2006년《심상》등단
작가회의 감사, 시우주낭송회회장
시집『스타카토』
lhspoet@naver.com

Writing on the Picture of Butterflies

Heo Young-suk

During that season I believed all those which stood in unattainable places were paths of flowers. I once loved flowers hearing the outcries of mature flowers. As I loved flowers, wings sprouted; the things within flowers and those outside became a palpitating center. Since I communicated with pistils, the places where I sat folding wings were all flower places.

Though I flew over the flower paths, carrying pistils did not necessarily mean harboring lovely powder in the bosom.

The flower poison I couldn't perceive though I had compound eyes hurt my wings. And I land over Mt Da in the distant south. The daytime moon closely follows me. In the teakettle, water boils. Fly freely outside flowers, but don't adore and hover over pistils. A man who came here with hurt wings long ago is writing over the vacant sky with warm brush-tips.

나비그림에 쓰다

허 영 숙

닿을 수 없는 곳에 있는 것은 다 꽃길이라 믿었던 시절 득음한 꽃들의 아우성에 나도 한때 꽃을 사모하였다 꽃을 사모하니 저절로 날개가 돋아 꽃 안의 일도 꽃 밖의 일도 두근거리는 중심이 되었다 꽃술과 교감했으므로 날개 접고 앉은 자리가 모두 꽃자리였다

꽃길을 날아다녔으나 꽃술을 품었다고 흉금에 다 아름다운 분粉을 지닌 것은 아니었다

겹눈을 가지고도 읽지 못한 꽃독에 날개를 다치고 먼 남쪽 다산에 와서 앉는다 낮달이 다붓하게 따라온다 주전자에는 찻물이 끓고 *꽃 밖에서 훨훨 날아다니고 꽃술을 사모하여 맴돌지는 말아라 오래 전 날개를 다치고 이곳에 먼저 와서 앉았던 사람이 더운 붓끝으로 허공에 쓰고 있다

* 정약용의 시 "나비그림에 쓰다" 에서 인용

POME

허영숙
2006년 《시안》 등단
시집 『바코드』
bluerain9341@hanmail.net

Empyema

Gim Yeung-chan

Shame on me;
I was suffering from empyema.

That was not really so shameful
In truth I wanted to go to S University.
Shame! My dream was to go to S University.
Shame! That was the maximum task
For a 16-year-old lad--a great dream.
Shame! I could only get 25 points in math;
This shameful empyema!
My only excuse was the empyema.
Proffering empyema as an excuse,
I entered a college where math was not mandatory.
Shame! I wrote joking poetry
Offering empyema as an excuse.

I became gradually accustomed to posing as a poet.
Shamefully, I came to think that
That was the beginning of good farming.

축농, 축농증

김 영 찬

챙피하게도 축농, 충/농증을 앓고 있었다

그것이 챙피한 게 아니라
에스대학이라는 델 가고 싶었다
챙피하게도 에스대학에 가려는 게 꿈이었다
챙피하지만 그것이 열여섯 젊은 녀석의 최대의 과제
기껏 원대한 꿈, 이었다
창피하게도,
챙 넓은 챙 아니 챙/피하지도 못하고
수학을 25점 밖에 받지 못했다 창피하게도
이놈의 축농증!
충 농증 핑계를 댈 수밖에 없었다
챙피하지만 축농증을 핑계로 수학이 없는 대학에 들어갔다
챙피하게도 축농증을 핑계로 대학에서 충충
농弄의 시를 썼다

창피하지만 차츰 시인 흉내를 내는데 익숙해져 갔다
창피하긴 하지만 그것이 축, 농農
잘된 농사일의 시작이었다고 생각하게 되었다

POME
김영찬
2002년 계간《문학마당》
시집『불멸을 힐끗 쳐다보다』외 1권
tammy3m@hanmail.net

Decalcomania

Bak Jong-in

I fold memory into halves.

Barley blooms.
Childhood ripens of itself.
The poor lunch-box struggles over the hill of hunger.
The season, racing without a chance to look back, whirls around in fury.
Faces bloating yellowish lie down in the barley field.
Lepers hide in the barley field;
The struggling barley field of hunger suffers ringworms and yellowish snivel.

I spread out the folded memory.

It's a different pattern
The flags of importing and exporting countries off the latches
Barley becomes dollars and apartments
A rosy season blooms in bubbles
The prodigal son is returning home into the foreign exchange crisis
The turbulent world lies down like barley

The barley dishes which evaporated stealthily
Go over the new barley hill, sporting
A brand name of health food
The barley buffet made from barley of memory pricks the old age' s futile heart
The home left alone calls loud
It' s empty-handed.

데칼코마니

박 종 인

추억을 반으로 접는다

보리가 핀다
유년기가 절로 익는다
맹물도시락이 보릿고개를 허청허청 넘고
돌아볼 겨를 없이 달려온 세월이 회오리에 휘감기고
누렇게 뜬 얼굴들 보리밭에 드러눕고 문둥이가 보리밭에 숨는다
힘든 보릿고개 버짐이 피고 누런 콧물이 흐른다

접었던 기억을 펼친다

무늬가 다르다
수출입국 깃발이 빗장을 열고
보리는 달러가 되고 아파트가 된다
거품으로 피어오르는 장밋빛 계절
외환위기 환난 속으로 탕자들이 귀향한다
어지러운 세상이 보리처럼 눕고 슬며시 증발했던 보리밥
건강식이라는 꼬리표 달고
신보릿고개 넘는다

보리밥뷔페 추억의 보리 까스라기처럼 노년기 빈 가슴을 찌른다
혼자 남은 고향이 부른다
빈손이다

POME
박종인
제9회 산림문화작품공모전 대상
《애지》등단
p7a7r7k@hanmil.net

New Construction

Bok Gi-wan

Bulky demolition equipment comes near,
Making deafening roars.
The gingko tree stands firm
Within the enclosure about to be demolished.
O yes, the magpie is the constructor.
A magpie, shorn of feathers and with haggard looks,
Is busy moving construction materials for several days.
The magpie designed the sky as its roof.
That house does not get wet with rain, even in a rain-shower,
Dead branches having been woven together like our solid love.
I' m ashamed of the expert knowledge
I acquired during the times I lived like an excavator
Demolish your own desire before removing an old house.
The magpies that build houses in trees
Without a piece of land babbled all day long.
After my hair dwindled, I saw the magpie' s nest
That I could not see when the wood was dense.
In between branches that could not cut the wind,
The magpie' s nests let cares and worries escape.
Sunbeams glittering like precious stones filled the house.
Who could have taught them how to design?
The lovely nest that can hold
The sun, moon, and star.

신축 공사

복 기 완

육중한 철거 장비 굉음 울며 다가오는데
집 철거 앞둔 울안의 은행나무 끄떡없다
오호라 ! 까치가 건축쟁이지
털도 다 빠지고 윤기마저 없는 까치 한마리
며칠째 자재 물어 나르기 바쁘다
까치는 하늘을 지붕으로 설계했으니
삭정이와 삭정이, 마치 너와 나의 튼튼한 사랑처럼
엮어져 큰 비가 내려도
그 집은 비에 젖지 않는다
포클레인처럼 살아온 그 세월에
내가 배운 전문 지식이 부끄럽다
낡은 집 철거하는 일보다 네 욕심 먼저 철거하라
땅 한 평 없이 나무에 집을 짓는 까치들이
한나절을 쪼잘거렸다
내 머리 숱 작아지고, 보았다
숲이 울창할 땐 보이지 않던 까치집
바람도 걸리지 않는 나뭇가지 가지 사이로
근심 걱정 솔솔 다 빠져 나간 까치집에
보석처럼 반짝이는 햇살이 소복이 담겨 있다
도대체 저 설계를 누가 가르쳐 주었을까
해와 달과 별을 담을 수 있는 아름다운 집

POME

복기완
《시와 창작》등단
시집『기벼움에 대한 애착』외
시와 창작 작가회 감사,
월간《광장》편집위원.

Implant

Han Sang-rim

Old teeth slumber in the film.
Unlike the pupa, which crawls out
Dreaming of flying,
The milk tooth that has hardened
Coming through the tender gums, or
The wisdom tooth that passed through the hard gap
On the day of first love-ache--
The blue gums that cannot renew or be filled again
Tend yellowed teeth
Putting them to sleep cuddling in the cold light.

The first day she had her wisdom tooth plucked out,
Her tongue nursed the void
Where it had been removed;
She consoled herself about the one lost tooth.
And then one, two, three, four and still more were
Replaced by new teeth, which luckily
Appeared stronger than genuine teeth.
And then, six molars devoid of nerves,
Propped up by loose screws and
Biting into x-ray light,
Are now simply simpering.

임플란트

한 상 림

오래된 치아들은 필름 속에서 잠을 잔다
금방이라도 꿈틀꿈틀 기어 나오며
비상을 꿈꾸는 애벌레나, 혹은
여린 잇몸 뚫고서 단단해졌을 젖니와
첫사랑 가슴앓이 시작되던 날
단단한 틈새를 뚫고 나오던 사랑니처럼
다시 새로워지거나 채워질 것이 없는
무른 잇몸은, 누런 니들을 다독이며
찬 불빛 받아 안고 가지런히 누에잠을 재운다

맨 처음 사랑니 하나 빼고 온 날
뿌리 뽑혀나간 물컹한 그 자리 혀로 다독이며
괜찮다, 괜찮다, 그깟 하나쯤이야, 달랬었다
그리고 둘, 셋, 넷중…중요롭던 자리에서 스스로
무너져가는 어금니들을 빼내고 새 니를 심었더니
진짜보다 더 단단해 보였다. 그러던,
신경줄기 없는 여섯 개의 어금니들이 삐뚤빼뚤
헐렁한 나사옷을 입고
엑스레이 불빛 깨물고 물어뜯다가
멋쩍은 듯 웃고 있다

POME

한상림
《예술세계》시 등단, 《시와 창작》 수필 등단
글마루문학동인 아토포스 동인 회장
서울시장 표창(공로), 복숭아문학상 수상
시집『따뜻한 쉼표』

Immortality

I Won-sik

Flowers bloom and fade
at the dumb song by the wind.

The wind smoke that cannot possess
even the illegitimate fragrance.

The vague sound of waves (1),
the flower petals must be about to fall.

* In Buddhism Buddha' s words are compared to the sound of tides.

불후不朽

이 원 식

바람의 무언가無言歌에
꽃들은 피고 진다

내연內緣의 향기조차
소유할 수 없는 풍연風煙

꽃잎이 지려나 보다
어렴풋한
파도소리*

* 불가(佛家)에서 부처님 말씀을 조수(潮水)소리에 비유한 말. 해조음(海潮音).

POME

이원식
2005년 《월간문학》 시조 등단
《불교문학》 시 등단
시집 『누렁이 마음』 외 2권

If

No Un-mi

If you, a father with a paunch,
harboring palpitating tears of compassion
and raw lives,
became a mother
If you cannot give birth because
you don't have the necessary delivery kits
If you are dying with the aging fetus
If you put a 36-month-old fetus on a diet
If someone grinds a knife for you each night
If he parts your round belly and bursts out laughing
If blood-colored waters fill up the room
and there you play water polo as a fetus
If all men's bellies become parturient
If even today
a man, sitting sedately, hugs the quilt crying
If I smoke a cigarette, sitting naked on the couch
If I'm the father of all fetuses
saying don't worry, don't worry.

만약에

노 운 미

아직도
풀지 못한 낡은 자루慈淚
날 것의 생들이 팔딱이는 배 불룩한
아빠인 네가 엄마가 된다면
출산용품이 없어서 아기를 낳을 수 없다면
늙어가는 태아와 함께 죽어가는 것이라면
삼십 육 개월 된 태아를 다이어트 시킨다면
엄마인 너를 위해 밤마다 칼을 갈고 있다면
둥근 너의 배를 가르며 폭소를 한다면
핏빛 양수가 방안 가득 차오른다면
그 속에서 태아로 수구를 한다면
모든 남자들의 배가 만삭이 된다면
오늘도,
다소곳이 앉은 남자가 이불을 감싸 안고 울고 있다면
침대에 걸터앉은 나체의 내가 담배를 피우고 있다면
걱정하지 마! 걱정 마! 하는 내가 모든 태아들의 아비라면

POME
노운미
여주 출생
2006년 《시선》 등단
시집 『유령으로 나는 서 있네』
profond@hanmail.net

When One Can See Ieodo Island

Yang Geum-hui

When winds blew and waves surged,
Jeju women worried about their husbands and sons
who had gone to sea,
watching white surfs splashing over the rocks.

Jeju women had to see Ieodo Island by all means
when several days and months had elapsed.

Ieodo Island, Iedo Island,
an island of plenty and comfort
that must be somewhere halfway along the Haenam route.

Jeju women believed in the island,
an island free from pain or hunger and
full of lotus flowers,
that must be somewhere far over that ocean,
an island that would free their husbands and sons from pain.

An underwater reef 4 to 6 meters below the surface
that can be seen from tall billows
an island fishermen would see on the verge of death
an island that gave solace to Jeju women.

Those who were looking for Ieodo Island,
across and beyond legends,
have finally built the Ieodo Island Marine Science Base,
a lotus base that has bloomed out of Jeju women' s wish,
standing tall and erect over the endless ocean.

이어도가 보일 때는

양 금 희

바람이 불어 파도가 치면
바위에 부서지는 흰 물결 보며
제주 아낙들은 고기잡이 떠난
남편과 아들을 걱정했다

며칠이 지나고
몇 달이 가면
기어이 제주 여인들은
이어도를 보아야만 했다

해남길의 반쯤 어딘가에 있을
풍요의 섬 이어도
안락의 섬 이어도

제주여인들은 섬을 믿었다
저 바다 멀리 어딘가에 있는
아픔도 배고픔도 없는 연꽃 가득한 섬
남편과 아들을
고통에서 해방시키는 섬을

높은 파도에서만 모습 보이는
수면 아래 4,6미터 수중암초
어부들이 죽음에 임박해서나 봤을 섬
제주 여인들에게 위안을 주던 섬

이어도를 찾던 사람들이
전설을 넘어
마침내 이어도 해양과학기지를 세웠다
망망대해에 우뚝 선
제주여인의 기원으로 피어난 연꽃 기지

POME
양금희
제주인뉴스 편집국장
이어도문학회 회장
시집 『행복계좌』

Ieodo Island, and Waiting

Kim Eun-sook

The old hack–berry tree at the entrance to the village
Arduously upholds its neck
Which is getting longer weary with waiting.

The child,
In the darkness following sunset,
Stands waiting for news about him who has gone to sea.

In his mind,
He can see Ieodo Island
Which has risen above the calm waves.

The yearning for the island grows day after day.
A stone the size of a fist falls into the heart.
Mother and Father have not returned
Since they went away.

The child,
With the maturing season,
Learned the unforeseen port' s way of waiting
And encountered the sea eye to eye
Till he became an adult.

At last,
Ieodo Island dropped suddenly
And the waiting ceased.

이어도, 그리고 기다림

김 은 숙

마을 어귀의 늙은 팽나무
기다림에 지쳐 길어지는 목을
힘겹게 치켜들고 있다.

해가 넘어간 어둠 속에서
아이는,
훌쩍 바다로 떠난 이의
소식을 기다리며 서 있고

마음속에서는
잔잔한 파도 위로 솟은 섬
이어도가 보인다
가도 가도 그리운 섬
심장에 주먹만한 돌 하나 툭,
떠나 돌아오지 않는
어머니 아버지……

아이는,
세월이 익어 가면서
기약 없는 포구의 기다림을 배워
바다와 눈싸움을 하였다
어른이 되기까지

마침내
톡
이어도가 떨어지고
기다림도 사라졌다

P O M E
김은숙
월간《스토리문학》 등단
풀잎문학회 회장역임
제주문인협회 간사

Autumn Shuts the Door

Gim Min-cheol

I'm a reed warbler; standing on a branch a step higher, I look down at the empty nest. In one corner of the room warmth still remains. I've made a living from the green foliage, using the shade as my quilt. A few days later I heard the lovely song of the cuckoo. There may have been a loudspeaker where the cuckoo sang. The sound spread out far into the distance like green light. The sky was a huge loudspeaker in those moments; even caterpillars came outside to listen, crawling into the mouths of children still barefoot. To that extent the house became narrower and narrower. We had to abandon pieces of furniture one after another. Cloud was one of the items I threw out. Once the clouds heldthe children like a garbage bag, taking them to a very high place. I become sad in the morning when it rains. This afternoon the cuckoo's song has receded, and a cool breeze brushes. My mouth waters smelling the wind after a few days of loss of appetite.

I'll try to live on. I get strength in my wing feathers. Autumn will soon close the door of the nest for me.

가을이 문을 잠그고

김 민 철

나는 개개비입니다 한 계단 정도 높은 나뭇가지에 서서 텅 빈 둥지를 내려다보지요 아직 아랫목에는 온기가 남아 있어요 푸른 잎사귀를 살림살이로 마련하고 그늘을 이불로 덮고 살았지요 며칠 후 뻐꾸기의 고운 노랫소리가 들려왔지요 뻐꾸기가 있는 자리엔 마이크가 있었는지 몰라요 소리가 파란 빛깔처럼 멀리멀리 퍼져 나갔죠 하늘은 거대한 스피커 같았지요 그 시간엔 송충이들도 바깥으로 나와 귀 기울이다 아직 맨살로 버티는 아이들의 입속으로 기어들어 가기도 했죠 그만큼 집안이 점점 좁아지기 시작했지요 살림살이들을 하나 둘 내다버릴 수밖에 없었죠 구름은 내가 버린 쓰레기 중에 하나이지요 저 구름이 쓰레기봉지처럼 아이들을 꽉 묶어 너무 높은 곳으로 떠난 적도 있지요 비가 오는 아침은 서글퍼져요 뻐꾸기 노랫소리가 사라진 오후 시원한 바람이 부네요 며칠 입맛이 없더니 바람 냄새에 드디어 침이 고이네요 나도 살아 볼게요 이제 날개깃에 힘이 생겨요 가을이 곧 내 대신 둥지의 문을 걸어 잠그겠지요

POME

김민철
1981년 서울 출생
2012년 《문화일보》 신춘문예 시당선

Winter Tree

Kim Il-ung

Though my body has not grown suddenly bigger,
my clothes feel uncomfortable.

The hill' s shadow flickering at the paling sunlight--
If it meets the wild wind with a spring-weary body,
it must take off its only clothing out of fear.

On a day when my humble neighbors collapse,
cut down by the knife of a wind, and even the familiar joy
and pain snap up, I see you struggling at the end of a thready knot.

Pain and suffering that come easily and disappear without a trace do not have enough sap left to endure the flagellation, but wait for a thaw in the frozen land.

A shadow that met a premature death while witnessing
with a naked body the wailing of broken arms and legs
is feeble and hardly audible.

The blue heaven and earth have closed their eyes and ears.

겨울나무

김 일 웅

갑자기 몸이 커진 것도 아닌데
입은 옷 부담스럽다

창백해진 햇볕에 이죽거리는 산 그림자
봄 때 젖은 몸으로 사나워진 바람 만나면
두려움에 홑옷이라도 벗어야 한다

내 작은 이웃들이 칼바람에 힘없이 쓰러지고
손에 익은 기쁨과 아픔마저 후두둑 부러진 날
실낱같은 마디 끝에서 용쓰는 너를 본다.

쉽게 찾아와 흔적 없이 사라지는 苦
매질 견디며 凍土 속 해빙을 기다리기엔
남은 수액水液 그리 넉넉지 않다

부러진 팔다리 곡성에
알몸으로 노래 부르는 요절한 그림자
스치는 기력조차 쇠잔해 들릴 듯 마는 듯
창천蒼天 천지도 눈귀 감아 버렸다.

POME

김일웅
월간 《문학세계》 등단
시집 『별을 찾아가는 여행』 외 1편 황희문학상수상
tiger7668@hanmail.net

Go Gyeong-suk_Gim Seong-su_Sin Hyeon-bok

Moon Chun-sik_Choe Eul-won_Yun Jun-gyeong_Na Seok-jung

An Gap-seon_Mun Hui-bong

Park Su-geol_U Ok-ja_An Ji-myeong_Jeong Ji-yong

I Tae-un_Bak Dong-nam_I Sa-rang

Oh Yeong-rok_Jeong Mi-gyeong_Choe Chang-sun

Ye Si-won _Seo Young-yong_U Ae-ja_Jo Young-hwan

Gim Gyeong-sik_Gim Gyeong-gon

Gim Young-eun

Poems of 100 Major
Contemporary Korean Poets

chapter 04

Go Gyeong-suk_Gim Seong-su_Sin Hyeon-bok

Moon Chun-sik_Choe Eul-won_Yun Jun-gyeong_Na Seok-jung

An Gap-seon_Mun Hui-bong

Park Su-geol_U Ok-ja_An Ji-myeong_Jeong Ji-yong

I Tae-un_Bak Dong-nam_I Sa-rang

Oh Yeong-rok_Jeong Mi-gyeong_Choe Chang-sun

Ye Si-won _Seo Yeung-yong_U Ae-ja_Jo Young-hwan

Gim Gyeong-sik_Gim Gyeong-gon

Gim Young-eun

Subversive Landscape

Go Gyeong-suk

The hapless evening
Spreads a blood-colored twilight over the sky
And runs away.
The exhausted hills extend their limbs
And sink into the sea.
Those upholding the darkness
Have narrowed down the landscape's peripheries.
The sound of the salty wind piercing the body of a goby
Slipping through the net's meshes
Hits the forest and the door, and heads towards the field.
The crops, all day friendly to the light,
Cover their bodies head to foot with white vinyl
And put up resistance.
There is zero light all around,
And no civilization.
Will the night be long?
Occasionally a few crabs crawl out of the silt field
On a scouting mission and then disappear.
Along the tortuous coastline
The drunken waves repeat themselves again and again.
But is it the sea alone that staggers?
The silt rocks, deeply pensive,
All night submit to the cockeyed brawl
And wait for the morrow in the subversive landscape.

불온한 풍경

고 경 숙

불우했던 저녁은
하늘에 핏빛 노을을 불 지르고 달아났다
기진맥진한 산들이 사지를 늘어뜨리고
바다로 빠진다
어둠을 옹호하는 것들은
풍경의 외곽을 좁혀 왔다
짠내 나는 바람이 그물코를 빠져나와
내걸린 망둥어 몸통을 관통하는 소리
숲을 치고, 문짝을 치고, 들판을 향한다
종일 빛에 우호적이던 작물들은
흰 비닐을 머리끝까지 뒤집어쓰고 저항했다
사방은 이제 명도 제로
문명은 없다
밤이 길까?
가끔 갯벌 밖으로 능쟁이 몇 마리
정찰 나왔다 사라진다
지리멸렬한 해안선을 따라 술 취한 파도
한소리또하고한소리자꾸또해도
휘청이는 것이 바다뿐이랴
속 깊은 갯바위, 밤새 그 주사酒邪 받으며
불온한 풍경 속에서 아침을 기다리는…

P O M E
고경숙
계간 《시현실》 등단
수주문학상 운영위원 ,예총 기획위원
수주문학상
시집 『모텔 캘리포니아』 『달의 뒤편』 외 1권

Formula for Walking

Gim Seong-su

My illness is building a pyramid,
A grave for my walk to enter and lie down.
The two legs that have raced for 34 years
Have been trapped into an acute rheumatism.
The word for knee joint has been erased from my dictionary.
Since the left foot extends three spans
And the right foot four spans, when I walk,
I lance my walking stick into a spot 5 spans away,
Thereby completing the Pythagorean theorem.
The walk accomplished by these three apexes
Are more complete than a walk achieved by two points.
So I've never stumbled for 15 years.
I walk by wielding my stick ahead and behind me,
Crossing myself in that manner.
I recitelike a prayer
"Thesis, antithesis and synthesis""
Along my steep or tortuous path of affliction
And submit myself to the way of going around or evading,
And my gait becomes solid and steady.
What joint could have been deleted from the dictionary today?
I lay my mind in the pyramid that has been built 60%
By laying bricks of the joint one after another.
The whole universe is visible through the crevice of the 40%
That has yet to be covered.

걸음의 공식

김 성 수

내 병이 피라미드를 만들고 있다
걸음이 들어가 누울 무덤이다
서른하고도 네 해를 질주한 양다리가
급성류머티즘에 갇혀
내 사전에는 무릎관절이란 단어가 삭제되었다
왼발이 세 뼘 뻗으면 오른발이 네 뼘을 뻗는 통에
나는 다섯 뼘 자리에 지팡이를 찍어
피타고라스의 정리를 완성한다
이 세 꼭짓점으로 이루는 걸음은
두 점으로 이루는 걸음보다 완전하여
나는 열다섯 해 동안 넘어지지 않았다
지팡이를 앞뒤로 짚는 내 걸음은 성호를 긋는다
가파르거나 굴곡진 고난의 길에서
정합반正反合, 정반합正反合을 기도문처럼 외며
돌아가거나 비껴가는 순응에 귀의할 때
내 걸음은 단단해진다
오늘은 사전에서 어느 관절이 지워졌을까
한 장 한 장 관절의 벽돌을 얹어
육 할을 쌓아올린 피라미드에 마음을 눕힌다
아직 덮지 않은 사 할의 틈으로 온 우주가 보인다

P O M E

김성수
2003년《현대시》등단
난시동인회장, 다시올문학 편집위원
시집『걸음의 공식』

Bitter Affection

Sin Hyeon-bok

Mother, you are drying them for many a time.

Pepper spreads in grandmother' s room.
Half-dry, they emanate thick bitter smell.
One can see some tender ones here and there,
The really dry ones are contained in the bag.
I asked why they were not being dried in the lower room,
She laughingly retorts, "just to chase out grandmom' s smell
Which wouldn' t go though they kept the door open so long.

So it' s like that. These red things that filled the room
Resembles toiling in the husband' s house.
So she has been drying the painful young widow' s days.
But then the dried things in that bag,
They are all sorrow.

If one dried and pounded sorrow,
It' d be bitter affection,
A spice that whets taste.

How many more times do you have to bring them in
To dry, Mother?

매운 情

신 현 복

어머니, 몇 물째 따다 말리시는 건가요

할머니 방에 고추가 널려 있다
반쯤 마른 채 매운 냄새 짙게 풍기고 있다
듬성듬성 짓무른 것도 보이고
바싹 마른 것들은 푸대에 담겨 있다
아랫방에다 말리면 되는데 싫어 여쭸더니
창문을 그렇게 열어 뒀는데도
돌아가신 할머니 냄새 도무지 가시지 않아
그 냄새 쫓느라고, 슬쩍 웃으신다

그렇구나, 방안 가득 이 붉은 것들 한때는
시퍼렇던 시집살이로구나
눈물겹던 청상의 여름날들을
이렇게 꼬들꼬들 말리고 계셨구나
그럼 푸대 속 저 마른 것들
하, 설움이구나

설움도 곱게 말려 빻으면 매운 情,
맛 돋우는 양념이 되는구나

몇 물을 더 따다 말려야 끝물인가요, 어머니

POME
신현복
1964년 충남 당진 생
2005년《문학.선》등단
시집『동미집』
cl_stone@hanmail.net

Absent

Moon Chun-sik

In this late night again.

God is again absent.
Every grieving one is firing a machine-gun
indiscriminately towards the sky.

God' s old vinyl floor is riddled with holes,
the leaking light becomes stars and cling to the darkness.

Empty cartridges scattering over the land form mounds;
In the wasteland only pieces of vinyl flutter.

People have no more target to shoot at.
They turn towards the only people surviving on earth.

Paper money whirls as scrap paper;
Economic bombshells fall.
Wherever life' s gun-smoke blooms
Close combats take place.
Oil wells are burning with fire
set by starving beasts.
The homeless, hit by a bullet,
fumbles about limping.

A church stands intact
by a demolished hospital.
In this land God is still absent.

부재중

문 춘 식

오늘도 늦은 밤

하느님은 또 부재중이다.
원성이 높은 사람들 저마다 기관총 들고
하늘 향해 무차별 난사한다.

오래 된 하느님의 비닐장판 구멍으로 가득하고
새 나오는 불빛, 별 되어 어둠에 걸린다.

땅위에 흩어지는 탄피 무덤을 이루고
황폐의 땅엔 비닐조각만 펄럭인다.

사람들은 더 이상 조준 할 것이 없어서
지구상 유일하게 살아 있는 사람들
겨냥하기 시작했다

휴지가 되어버린 화폐가 날리고.
경제의 폭탄이 떨어지고
삶의 포연이 피어나는 곳 마다 백병전을 벌이고 있다.
굶주림에 지친 짐승들이 저지른 방화에 유전이 불타고
총에 맞은 노숙자, 절룩거리며 방황하고 있다.

부서진 병원 옆에 교회만 멀쩡한데
지금 이 땅에 하느님은 여전히 부재중

POME

문춘식
1978년 《현대문학》 2회 추천
교원문학 등단
시집 『짓거리』 『사랑아 사람아』 외 3권

History Upon A Table

Choe Eul-won

A family eat meat at a road-side meat shop.
There's a dogma in the household head's scissoring.
The children sparkle like coke bubbles.
They are happy as a mouth wide open.
They munch on the sunbeams.
In one hidden corner, a middle-aged man and woman,
Apparently involved in an extramarital affair,
Fret like ripening time;
Uneasy each time the meat is turned,
They love each other each time they chew.
The two tables are Hebraism and Hellenism, respectively.
The system and the non-system, Logos and Eros.
All things of the world sit on one or the other of the tables,
Want to sit, or are in process of changing seats.
The husband and wife raise their voice suddenly.
It's a war. The children cry. It's an arbitration.
The landlady intercedes. It's an interference.
The man and wife, watching, have eye-contact with them
And quickly look away. It's ethics or ideology.
The restaurant doors open. On the table the two nations
Have left, bones gather in a heap. It's history.

It' s a tower of ox bones. The sunlight passes
Through the abandoned things.
As another century unfolds following a thorough scouring,
A high–class foreign car enters the yard.
A hungry dog of nomadism prowls about.

식탁 위의 역사

최 을 원

길가 고깃집에서 한 가족이 고기를 먹는다
가장의 가위질엔 도그마가 있다 아이들은
콜라 거품처럼 보글거린다 한껏 벌린
입만큼 행복하다 햇살이 오물오물 씹힌다
구석진 자리엔 한눈에도 불륜인 중년 남녀
익는 시간만큼 초조하고
뒤집는 횟수만큼 불안하고 뜯는 순간만큼 사랑한다
두 식탁은 헤브라이즘과 헬레니즘이다
제도권과 비제도권이다 로고스와 에로스다
세상 모든 것들이 두 테이블 중 한 곳에 앉아 있거나
앉아 있고 싶거나, 자리를 바꾸는 중이다
부부가 갑자기 언성을 높인다 전쟁이다 아이들이
운다 중재다 주인여자가 말린다 간섭이다
쳐다보던 남녀가 웃다가 눈이 마주치자
얼른 시선을 돌린다 윤리 혹은 이념이다
식당문이 열리고 두 민족이 빠져나간 식탁에는
뼈다귀들이 수북이 쌓여있다 역사다
우골탑이다 버려진 것들 사이로
햇살이 지나간다

말끔한 행주질로 또 한 세기가 열릴 때
고급 외제차 한 대 들어서는 마당,
유목의 개 한 마리 허기져 어슬렁거리고 있다

POME
최을원
2002년《문학사상》등단
시집『계단은 잠들지 않는다』
chldmfdnjs@daum.net

Two Persons

Yun Jun-gyeong

Two persons are walking along the road;
They hold each other's hand.

The woman's back is bent;
The man hangs on a stick.

The woman walks half a step ahead;
The man walks half a step behind.

The woman appears to lead the man;
The man seemsto escort the woman.

Their hair is grey;
It's hard to tell how far they've walked.

They sit on a bench;
They may have decided to take some rest.

두 사람

윤 준 경

두 사람이 길을 가고 있다
서로 손을 잡았다

여자는 허리가 굽고
남자는 지팡이를 짚었다

여자는 반 발짝 앞서 걷고
남자는 반 발짝 뒤에서 걷는다

여자가 남자를 이끄는 것도 같고
남자가 여자를 에스코트하는 것도 같고

얼마나 걸어왔는지 머리가 다 세었다

쉬었다 가기로 했는지
벤치에 앉는다

POME
윤준경
1994년《한맥문학》신인상
1995년 교자문원 3회 추천완료
시집『나 그래도 꽤 괜찮은 여잡니다』『새의 습성』외 1권
june7590@hanmail.net

Water Drop

Na Seok-jung

Looking back,
I too was a water drop come from heaven.
I found an awkward place beneath the stone steps
and saw a dandelion living unperturbed.
Though my precarious life was nothing,
all the same I was a lonely water drop
wanting to fall and seep into you.
While I was staying awake through the night like an owl,
The nectar you bestowed on me
condensed and groomed eye-balls,
gathering over a tree leaf this morning.
It finally falls on the ground,
seeping into the thirsty earth and stirring a life.
That sea, which never dries moving from life to life,
is a large water drop too.
My water drop wants to add to the large water drop.
My meagre water drop
wants to seep into you totally.

물방울

나 석 중

돌이켜 보면
나도 하늘에서 온 물방울
돌계단 아래 옹색한 터를 잡고
어느 민들레 꿈적도 않고 사는 걸 보고
나의 위태한 삶은 아무것도 아니었지만
나도 하나의 외로운 물방울이어서
당신에게 떨어져 스미고 싶었네
내가 부엉이처럼 밤을 지새울 때
당신이 내려준 감로甘露는
서로 응집하여 눈동자를 키우고
또르르 나뭇잎 끝에 맺히는 이 아침
이윽고 땅에 떨어져 목마른
흙에 스미어 또 한 생명을 일으키네
생명에서 생명으로
항상 마르지 않는 저 바다도 큰 물방울
큰 물방울 보면 보태지고 싶은 내 물방울
당신에게 전적으로 스미고 싶은
나의
초라한 물방울

POME
나석중
전북 김제에서 태어남, 2005년 시집 『숨소리』로 작품활동
시 『촉감』 『물의 혀』 외 1편
"빈터" 명예동인
stonecenter@naver.com

They Don't Fear

An Gap-seon

Live like me, he says,
because a broken heart is a bluff.

Show me.

A hefty tractor
rolls over the wild grass
and tramples dandelions.

Pressed to death.
The dandelion is death.
A few days later,
the dandelion soars up,
pushing the wild grass.
Af if to show off,
a white flower is in bloom.
Though the plantain too has been trampled,
it says live like me
in a Buddhist meditation posture.

그들은 두려워 하지 않는다

안 갑 선

상심은 허세라며 자기처럼 살라 한다

보여달라

육중한 콤비롤러가
아스콘 덮고 민들레를 눌러 버렸다
압사
민들레는 죽었다
며칠 후
민들레가 아스콘 밀쳐내고 솟아올랐다 보란듯이
하얀 꽃 피웠다
질경이도 안전화에 짓밟혔지만
가부좌 틀고 자기처럼 살라 한다

P O M E
안갑선
2000년 월간《문예사조》등단
시집『통화중』『바지랑대와 손고동 소리』외 1권
천안낭송협회 부회장, 다시올문학기획이사
angabsun@hanmail.net

Love Play

Mun Hui-bong

The clouds with bubbling flesh
Are gathering into one cluster high in the air.
While the distance is getting shorter,
The body slides into another body.
A modest wine table must have been prepared,
Only the clinking of glasses breaks the silence.
There the mist blooms in clusters.
The silence is turning the alarm clock.
The sky is blue
Without the sound of rattling.
The collarbones' breathing becomes more harsh,
lying down in bed with a noise.
It must have made a ring with garden flowers.
Behind the bright spring sky,
The bare skin brushes against the starched quilt.

사랑 놀이

문 희 봉

뽀얗게 살이 오른 구름들이
상공에서 하나 되려나 보다
가까워지는 거리
한 몸이
다른 몸 속으로
미끄러져 들어간다
조촐한 술상이라도 차렸는가
잔 부딪치는 소리만이 고요를 깬다
뭉게뭉게 안개 피어오르는 그곳
괘종시계 돌리고 있는 침묵
덜그럭거리는 소리 없이
하늘이 파랗다
쇄골에 호흡이 가빠지고
다솜, 침대에 눕는 소리
풀꽃 반지 만들어 끼워 주나 보다
화사한 봄 하늘 뒤편
스삭스삭, 풀 먹인 이불 홑청에 맨 살갗
스치는 소리

POME
시인, 수필가, 《다시올문학》 평론 등단
素雲문학상, 대전문학상, 시집 『지천명의 노래』 『천리향』, 수필집 『아마릴리스』외 4권
대전문인협회 회장
mhb0902@nate.com

Springtime over Onchonchon River

Park Su-geol

The cherry trees lining the riverside
are chanting the Flower Sutra loudly.
The words, falling all at once,
Strike my shoulder like the bamboo stick.
The scales of the wave glittering in the Suyong Bay
are blue sutra phrases.
I clasp my hands to perceive the spring.
The people out to enjoy springtime read a page of the wave.
The railroad train that draws underlines
is actually reciting sutras.

As I listen intently,
There' s dark shade behind glowing things;
Brighter the light, darker the shade.

When I lift the shining spring' s wrap,
the river is seriously ill.

The right way to read the lucid sutra
spread over the Onchonchon River
is to allay the pain rather than to enhance the makeup.

When the short spring is over,
the Onchonchon River will stay idle all alone.

온천천의 봄

박 수 걸

천변에 늘어 선 벚꽃나무들
요란한 화엄경을 읊조린다
일시에 떨어지는 저 말씀들
죽비처럼 어깨를 친다
수영만에 반짝이는 물비늘도 푸른 경전
두 손 모아 봄을 읽는다
물결을 한 페이지씩 읽고 가는 상춘객들
밑줄을 그으며 달리는 열차도 경전을 읽고 간다

가만히 들여다보면
빛나는 것의 뒤는 더욱 어둡다
빛이 크면 그림자도 깊다

저 눈부신 봄의 포장을 벗겨 내면
그저 병이 깊은 하천

화려한 치장보다는
아픈 것을 위로하는 것이
온천천 맑은 경전을 보는 일이다

짧은 봄이 지고 나면
온천천은 혼자 앓을 것이다

POME
박수걸
경남 밀양 출생, 2008년 계간 《다시올문학》 등단
시집『내 속살 보여줄까』
다시올문학 운영위원
yasehoa@naver.com

A Pot of Cucumber Pickle

U Ok-ja

As soon as the lid lifts,
Love and hate pour out instantly
As if to explode.
A flock of time, gushing a pungent odor,
Soars and drifts;
It has barely maintained the abeyance of deviation.

I must really shed it.
Churning the salt water
The hard rumination of insurrection
As always holds its breath on its own
Ending with a whimper as if
"Cutting water with a knife!
Fungus blooming white.

The piercing taste
Splashed with boiling salt water
Swinging between despair and hope
Experiencing deep wound that shrinks and empties

For a poor dinner table
I take away the softening things.
On that bottom of the sealed pot

A yellowing ripe cucumber pickle

Will remain as a treasure.

Wu debuted through the Dasiall Literature. She is currently the principal of

Sau High School.

오이지 단지

우 옥 자

뚜껑이 열리자마자 폭발할 듯
일순 오열을 토하는 애증愛憎
일탈의 부력을 간신히 지탱해 온
군둥내 나는 시간들이
두웅 -둥 떠오른다

정말 버려야해
소금물속 휘저으며
모반謀反의 고된 되새김은
언제나처럼 제풀에 숨을 죽이며
'칼로 물베기' 로 싱겁게 끝날 걸
허옇게 핀 곰팡이

아삭아삭 곰삭은 맛은
펄펄 끓는 소금물 뒤집어 쓴 채
체념과 희망 속을 그네질하며
오그라져 비워지는
깊은 쓰라림

가난한 저녁상을 위하여
물러터진 것들을 건어 낸다
묶은 단지 저 밑바닥에

노랗게 익은 오이지 하나
보물처럼 남아 있으리

POME
우옥자
충남 서천 출생
《다시올문학》등단
'글샘' 문학동인
wooropa@hanmail.net

Shooting

An Ji-myeong

I unzip the rifle case.
A shotgun which has a higher hitting ratio than a pistol.
I aim it like Paul Newman aiming near the foot of the bad guy,
Holding the gun in one hand.

Hold!
Come forward a step.
Those who come here think theirs are shotguns.
Those who load viagras into the guns may have shotguns,
But they' re mostly pistols.
Come closer and spread legs wide as your shoulder;
Uphold the gun with one hand,
And pull the trigger in the direction of the target
When the line of sight is set and you fire the mothballs
The shells fly up,
Probably wetting your lower part.
Did you shudder?
Shake off the smell and erase the evidence.
Shooting is equal to an instinct to survive.
Close up the gun case and then you may step back.
If this were a military camp, you might earn a bonus furlough.

Those who correctly apply their instinct for hitting the target properly –

We' d offer you a ticket for firing in WC.

Good day.

A world where everybody aims the guns to survive.

So many pull the trigger aiming at so many targets.

The goals, large and small, that your set up

Are targets all alike.

사격

안 지 명

총집 지퍼를 열었다
권총보다 적중률이 좋은 장총
폴 뉴먼이 한손에 총을 쥐고 악당의 발아래를 겨누듯

잠깐!
한걸음 더 오시지요
여기 오시는 분들 자기 총이 장총이라고 생각들 하시는데
어쩌다 비아그라를 장전하신 분들은 장총이지만
대부분 권총이거든요
바짝 밀착 하시고 어깨만큼 다리를 벌리고
총을 한쪽 손으로 받치고
조준선정렬이 되면 과녁을 향해 방아쇠를 당기세요.
사격 중 좀약을 쏘시면 탄피가 튀겨
아랫도리가 젖을 수 있습니다
진저리 치셨습니까.
냄새를 탈탈 털어 증거를 지우십시오
발사는 생존본능
총집을 끝까지 닫으시고 물러나셔도 좋습니다
여기가 군대라면 포상휴가 감인데
명중본능을 발휘하신 선생님껜
저희 W.C 일회사격권을 드립니다.
안녕히 가십시오

온통 총을 겨누며 살자 본능의 세상
얼마나 많은 과녁을 향해 방아쇠를 당겼을까
살며 세웠던 크고 작은 목표들이 다 과녁이었다

POME
안지명
《다시올문학》작품활동
joyan57@naver.com

Medical Examination

Jeong Ji-yong

As I get my first stomach endoscope inspection,
I feel as if I've been deprived of my chastity.

While a foreign matter pricked my intestines,
All I could do was to endure it helplessly
with prolonged breathing.

In the space the thing roughly explored my virgin land,
They took off a piece without permission and
Asked me to pay additional bills and go home,
Just waiting for a later date.

For health's sake, I get a number ticket,
Wait, and pay a few bills
I find myself looking bizarre.

It's not just my age.

건강 검진

정 지 용

처음으로 위 내시경 검사를 받으며
어이없이 동정을 앗겨 버린 느낌이다.

이물질이 내 내장을 처음으로 쑤셔대는 동안
긴 호흡으로 맞서며 무기력하게 참아 내는 것이
내 한 일의 전부다.

내 처녀지를 탐색하는 물건이 휘젓고 다닌 공간에서
허락도 없이 조각을 띠어낸 그들은 참 당당하게
바용을 더 지불하고 그냥 가란다.
후일을 기다리란다.

건강을 위해서라며 번호표를 뽑아 기다려
화폐 몇 장 지불하고 뚜벅거리는 내 모양이 문득
참 낯설다.

나이 탓만은 아닌 듯도 하다마는…

POME

정지용
경기고등학교 졸업, 성균관대학교 국어국문학과 졸업
《다시올문학》 등단
시집 『계절의 초상』
susanin@nate.com

Stray Thoughts about Dongwha Temple

I Tae-un

In the temple site
Echoing with green sounds of reciting sutras,
Lovely are the hills, streams and drum sounds.
All alone, I wash my mind soiled with the rhinoceros' horn.

The lord sits on the lotus seat so serenely
The good visitors to the mountain temple are flustered.
The Buddha sits facing the wall for 1500 years.

The worldly matters are hasty
Because the inside is vacant.
If one adds a handful of epigrams from Sutta Nipata,
Avalokitesvara with thousand hands and eyes
Opens the tentacle of the lord.

* Lee made his début as a sijo poet through the Dasiall Literature.

동화사 단상桐華寺 斷想

이 태 운

푸른빛 독경讀經소리 어우러진 절터에
산 고와 물이 고와 북소리 절로 고와
홀로이 무소의 뿔처럼 때 낀 마음 씻는다

연좌蓮座에 앉으신 님 저리도 느긋한데
산사山寺의 선객善客들은 좌불안 야단법석
불보살 앉으신 자리 천오백 년 면벽 중

세상사 바쁜 것은 안內이 비어 분주할 뿐
먼발치 수타니파타의 경구 한 줌 더하면
고운님 촉수 틔우는 천수천안千手千眼 관세음

POME
이태운
1958.8.1 대구출생
경북대학교 법과대학 졸업
《다시올문학》시조 등단
(현)동부화재 부사장

The Tree That Revives after Death

Bak Dong-nam

An electric saw cuts the tree trunk.
I' m not sad at all
though my friends, standing together yet at intervals,
look with wet eyes.

If you ask me about my sins,
I' ve only sinned because I' ve loved winds,
Because I' ve embraced birds.

The burial of the tree is saintly.
The tree lives all its life standing and
lies down on earth only after death.

I revive there again;
That body devoid of hands and feet
was shamefully treated by grass and clay.

I want to revive after death
after being cut by an electric saw and chiselled by a plane.

If someone asks about my last wish,
I' ll say, I want to stay by you
as a book, as your couch, or a side post.

죽어서 다시 사는 나무

박 동 남

전기톱이 나무 밑동을 자른다
간격을 두고 함께 서 있던 친구들이
젖은 눈으로 바라보지만
나는 조금도 슬프지 않다

내게 죄를 묻는다면
바람을 사랑한 죄다
새들을 품어준 죄다

평생을 서서 살다가 죽어서야 땅에 눕는
나무의 순장은 성자처럼 거룩하다

손 발 다 떼어내고 남은 저 몸뚱이
풀에 흙에 부대끼어 끌려간
그곳에서 나는 다시 부활한다

기계톱에 잘리고 대패로 다듬어져
나는 죽어도 또 다시 살고 싶다

누군가 내게 마지막 소원을 묻는다면
한 권의 책으로 당신의 침대로
문설주로 당신 곁에 머물고 싶다

POME
박동남
2006년 경암 백일장 입상, 2008년 《다시올 문학》 등단
공저시집 『오월에 내린 눈』 『칸나가 붉게 피는 이유』
저서 『한국인의 명시 선집』 『불곡산의 미소』
dongnam52@naver.com

Self-portrait

I Sa-rang

My daughter in her puberty shoots out like a spring.
Lest I've screwed her up overmuch,
I release her a bit loose.
She climbs up to my crest and
repeatedly lifts and puts down my 60kg body.

Touting a name-plate as a mother,
I caress and hug her and then quietly say,
You must read a person's mind like a book.

Mother, do you read a person's mind well to get hurt?
She retorts and parries my remarks like ping-pong balls,
causing hot air to gush from my inside.
On such days, strangely, I hear
white hollyhocks breaking up in a corner of the yard.

My ear itches.
My mother, who cannot move even on all fours,
perhaps compalins about me, saying,
Bear a daughter like youself.

My mother, 49 years old,
holds my ears to clean them.

자화상

이 사 랑

사춘기 딸내미가 용수철처럼 툭 튕겨 나간다
너무 죄였나 싶어 느슨하게 풀어놓으면
정수리까지 올라와 육십 키로인 나를 번쩍 들었다
내려놓기를 반복하는데

명색이 어미라는 이름표를 달고
쓰다듬다가 안아 주다가 조용히,
사람의 마음도 책을 읽듯 읽어야 한다
엄마는 사람을 잘 읽어서 사람한테 상처 받아?

탁구공 치듯 똑딱똑딱 말을 받아치는데
속에서 뜨건 김이 푹푹 치솟는다
그런날은 엉뚱하게도 마당 귀퉁이에서
하얀 접시꽃 깨지는 소리가 들렸다

네 발로도 걷지 못하는 어머니
잔소리가 날아서 온 걸까
귀 속이 몹시 가렵다
이담에 너 닮은 딸 꼭 하나만 낳아 봐라

마흔아홉의 어머니가 내 귀를 열고 귀지를 파 주신다

POME
이사랑
2008년 《다시올문학》 등단
시와 창작동인
수주문학대상수상
poem2112@naver.com

Inchworm

Oh Yeong-rok

An inchworm was clinging onto my chest while I was taking a walk.
The way it stretched and contracted its body
it appeared to be measuring the distance with a stick.
The way it moved hurriedly to and fro,
it was measuring my mind.
It appeared to be measuring the height of virtues
I' ve piled up.
The way it waved its head as if to examine and confirm something
or hesitated for awhile,
it seemed to measure the magnitude of good and evil.
The busy inchworm now somehow stays still for awhile.
It must now find nothing to measure
before the good things I' ve done.
It stays still
as if all the good I' ve done
doesn' t measure up to its small height.

자벌레

오 영 록

산책길에 가슴께 붙은 자벌레 한 마리
몸을 쭉 늘렸다 옴츠렸다 하는 모습이
막대로 거리를 재는 듯하다
부지런히 오가는 모습이
아무래도 내 마음을 재고 있다
그동안 쌓아놓은
덕의 높이를 재는 모습인데
가끔은 머리를 휘저으며 무엇인가
확인하듯 살펴보기도
한참씩 망설이기도 하는 모습이
선악의 넓이를 재고 있다
한참을 오가던 자벌레
어찌된 일인지
한참을 움직이지 않는다
내가 행한 선 앞에서
잴 것이 없는 모양이다
저 작은 자벌레의
한 키도 될 수 없는
선행이었는지
꼼짝도 하지 않고 있다

POME
오영록
강원도 횡성출생
2010년《문학일보》신춘당선
《다시올문학》등단
cy3213@naver.com

Water' s Play

Jeong Mi-gyeong

Is it the law of gravity that rules us? Whether it' s the case or not, look at my body that soars airily in the spring wind, that gathers and roams about liltingly, flies with quietly erecting feathers with suddenly deepening glances, one day swooping down in accord with strict rules, casting a sad gaze towards lilac blossoms, kissing wax tree leaves briefly. Is it a love affair of the previous age, or my own?

The grandma' s grandma who softly embraced virgin Shimchong, sweet little sixteen, when in the middle of the ocean, billows roared and waves hit the ship' s prow. Whenever small fries frolic about, our family' s history is let loose. Do you see me guffawing with round eyes amid babbling laughter?

물의 유희

정 미 경

우리를 지배하는 것이 중력의 법칙이던가요? 그러거나 말거나 봄바람에 두둥실 날아오르는 제 몸을 보세요. 들까불며 뭉쳐 돌아다니다가 문득 깊어진 눈망울로 고요히 깃털을 세워 날아가기도 하는, 어느 날엔 지엄한 계율을 따라 우르르 휩쓸려 가기도 하는, 애잔하게 눈길 던진 배롱나무 꽃잎, 잠시 입맞춤한 쥐똥나무 잎, 선대의 연애인지 나의 연애인지.

대천 한가운데 풍랑 일고 물결 뱃전에 탕탕거릴 때 열다섯 처녀 심낭자를 포근히 감쌌다던 할머니의 할머니. 치어들이 노니는 곳마다 우리 가문의 내력을 풀어 놓아요. 동그래진 눈 재잘거림 속 깔깔 웃는 제 모습 보이나요?

POME
정미경
경북대 수학교육과 졸업
2011년 《다시올문학》 등단
yjmky@hanmail.net

Baby' s Cemetery in Omok Valley

Choe Chang-sun

In the deep valley at Dadaeri, Chungun-myon,
dead babies used to be buried in Baby' s Cemetery.

The young souls gathered
to build a cemetery of stones.

By the small grave
where baby cries were suppressed
with stones each night,
arrowroots get gross each year.

Where eco-valleys have appeared,
charcoal bath houses, markets,
folk restaurants and bustling people
have chased out the souls.
The homeless souls may be
shivering around the stone stupa and
the shrines over the hills.

When arrowroots bloom
and cuckoo cries come down to the village,
the breast of the mother who has lost her baby
is tinted more purple than azaleas.

오목골 애장터

최 창 순

청운면 다대리 깊은 산골짜기
아이가 죽으면 묻었다는 애기골

어린 영혼들 옹기종기 모여
돌무덤이 되었네

밤마다 흘러나오는 애기 울음을
돌로 눌러놓은 작은 무덤가
해마다 칡넝쿨이 우거졌네

생태마을이 들어서고
숯가마 찜질방 저잣거리 향토음식점
북적이는 사람들에게 밀려
갈 곳 잃은 영혼들
고개 넘어 돌탑 서낭당에 모여
오들오들 떨고 있을까

칡꽃이피고
뻐꾸기 울음이
마을로 내려오면,

자식 잃은 어미의 가슴은
진달래보다 붉게 물들었네

POME

최창순
2009년 계간 《다시올문학》 등단
영등포 문화원 민요판소리 연합회장, 다시올문학회 감사
현 양평 햇빛농장 경영
chsunch@hanmail.net

Grandma is Carried on a Baby Carriage

Ye Si-won

Okson's grandma goes to the market place;
Was injured badly in the knee in her youth

Okson's grandma, next door,
Who was totally illiterate,
Learned the alphabet from her son;
Her life-long illiteracy has warped her back.

Okson's grandmother is pulling the baby carriage.
She's passing through the market
Piled with grocery baskets.
The grandma has worked all her lifetime
With her broken knees and bent waist.

The grandma who wants to sit in the baby carriage
Is being carried in the baby carriage,
Her back being shoved by the season

할매가 유모차에 끌려간다

예 시 원

젊은 시절 골병이 무릎에 내려앉은
옥선이 할매 장 보러 간다.

낫 놓고 기역자도 모르던
옆집 옥선이 할매
아들에게 기역자를 배웠다.
평생 기역자만 기억했는지
등허리가 기역자로 굽었다.

옥선이 할매 유모차 밀고 간다.
시장통 쓸고 가는 할매
소꿉놀이 같은 바구니가 세월처럼 쌓여 있다.
할매는 평생 무릎으로 일하고
기역자 허리로만 일했다.

유모차에 앉고 싶은 할매
세월에 등 떠밀려 유모차에 끌려간다

POME

예시원
계간 《시와 사람》 시 등단,
《다시올문학》 소설 등단
시집 『브라보 유어 라이프』 외 1권
계간 《詩와늪》 편집주간

I Study the Feed-back Effect in the Eco-Park

Seo Yeung-yong

At midday when the sun is trapped in the cloud
The rainy season sets in today.
The Kang-seo Eco-Park swamp emits
The odor of the silt field.
The reeds soar high, spreading green leaves.
The small river fish create round ripples.
I realized my ignorance about life,
Studying two volumes of Introduction to Management.
Sitting on a bench, I ponder the feed-back effect of managing my life.
I pray that the study of management will melt
Into a military strategy and become an ecological nutrient like silt field.

Sitting on a bench in broad daylight
I learn the feedback principle of the Eco-Park
Where clear water flows through the silt field and
Fish frolic about.

Seo won the new writer's prize from the Dasiall Literature.
soeyoungyong@hanmail.net

생태공원에서 피드백효과를 공부한다

서 영 용

해가 구름에 갇힌 한낮
남부지방은 오늘부터 장마권에 들었다
강서생태공원 습지
뻘 냄새가 코끝을 건드린다
갈대들이 키를 돋으며 푸른 잎을 펼친다
작은 물고기들이 동그란 파문을 일으킨다
경영학원론 두 권을 공부하며
삶의 무지를 깨달았다
내 삶을 경영하는 피드백효과를 벤치에 앉아 고민한다
경영학이 손자병법에 녹아 뻘처럼 생태자양분이 되길 빈다

뻘밭에 맑은 물이 흐르고 물고기들이 노니는
생태공원의 피드백 속성을
한낮에 벤치에 앉아 배운다

POME
서영용
나주 출생, 세종대학교 경제학과 졸업
방송통신대학교 농학과 졸업
2010년 《다시올문학》 신인상
seoyoungyong@hanmail.net

Pulling the Dawn

U Ae-ja

At a wholesale fish market at Garakdong
Boxes of anchovies from East Sea, West Sea
and South Sear pour down through the dawn's dusk.
The silvery sea soars up into the sky.
Each time the dawn pulls the vacant sky,
the price list printed on the electronic board
jumps up like anchovies.
The tight air waves,
the fingers grasping and unfolding the vacant sky
speak rapidly parting the water current.
Hats heave over fingers gathering close,
Eyeballs suffering from corneitis fumble,
unable to read the words blossoming in the empty air.
Prices soar
while the thumb and the little finger flounder confusedly.
The fingers shoved by waves crumble like foam.
In the blood-shot eyes
the boxes of anchovies disappear in no time.
In the bursting heat,
life falls to the ground.
Glowering eyeballs, like starlight,
stick into the electronic board.
Even today she draws in the dawn of the dead anchovies
which escorts the silver sea.

새벽을 당기다

우 애 자

가락동 멸치 도매시장, 새벽어스름을 헤치고
동해, 서해, 남해에서 올라온 멸치가 상자째 쏟아진다
은빛 바다가 공중으로 솟구친다
새벽이 허공을 당길 때마다
전광판에 찍힌 가격표가 멸치처럼 튀어오른다
팽팽한 공기가 물결치고
허공을 쥐었다 폈다 하는 손가락들이
물살을 가르며 빠르게 말을 한다
빽빽하게 모인 손가락 틈에 앉은 331 모자,
각막연화증을 앓는 눈동자가
허공에 핀 말들을 읽지 못해 두리번거린다
파도치는 시세, 엄지와 검지가 방향을 잡지 못해
휘청거리는 사이
파고에 휩쓸린 손가락이 물거품처럼 스러진다
핏발 선 눈 밖으로 멸치 상자들이
삽시간에 사라져버린다
터질듯 부풀어 오르는 열기 속,
살아있는 목숨은 바닥에 떨어지고
부릅뜬 눈알이 별빛 되어 전광판에 꽂힌다
오늘도 그녀는 은빛 바다를 몰고 오는
죽은 멸치 떼의 새벽을 당긴다

P O M E

우애자
2010년《다시올문학》등단
aarym@naver.com

Wife' s Tears

Jo Yeung-hwan

When occasionally my wife weeps,
Sorrow resembles a fish with black eyes.
She weeps and weeps silently,
And at last throws up fish.
The flock of sorrows flap their fins energetically
Outside my wife' s body.
Even without putting her fingers in her throat
She regurgitates the fish.
Where on earth within her serene body
Could all those leaping sorrows have been lurking?
The fish that reveal the scales
That suddenly glitter along the water current,
The fish eyes that never close.
Sad is the sorrow that has forgotten death.

아내의 눈물

조 영 환

아내가 이따금 울 때
슬픔은 눈이 까만 물고기 같다
소리 없이 울고 울다가 드디어
그녀는 물고기를 토해낸다
세월의 뱃속에서 소화되기는커녕
아내의 몸 밖에서 힘차게
지느러미를 퍼덕이는 슬픔들
아내는 목구멍에 손가락을 넣지 않고도
물고기를 꾸역꾸역 토해낸다
잔잔한 아내의 몸 어디에
저렇게 펄펄 뛰는 슬픔이 있었을까
홀연히 물길을 따라 번쩍이는
비늘을 드러내는 물고기
감을 줄 모르는 물고기의 눈이
죽음을 잊은 슬픔이 슬프다

POME
조영환
동국대 국문학과 졸업
2009년《다시올문학》등단
흰뫼문학회 동인, 숭실고등학교 재직
jyh724@hanmail.net

Cafe Folkways

Gim Gyeong-sik

I can detect by instinct places which are good for waiting. While shaking off the cold air hanging onto the coat-tail, my face becomes ruddy with the light. A landscape wet with anxiety leans over a wooden table by a fireplace, hardly detected.

I was waiting alone. The rose hanging on the wall and the big magpie nest harboring electric bulbs instead of eggs have discolored, and now smell of dry grass. The singer still sings about old love, more than 30 years past, over an old music record.

Nothing has changed. Recalling his face for a moment, having pulled out a leaning chair with a shorter leg, remembering his sweet voice, and placating reversing memories, throwing two cubes of sugar into the coffee.

Holding a knife, shoving pieces of a well-done hamburger stake into the raw wound, until a pair of strange voices hover over low tones, and fade away into the wood fire.

The door did not open. Only birds, arriving late, occasionally came to the window, asking for direction in the dim light.

* Note. Cafe Folkways is located in Gochon-myon, Kimpo City.

카페 포크웨이즈Folkways

김 경 식

나는 습관적으로 기다리기에 좋은 자리를 알고 있다 외투자락에 묻어온 냉기를 떨어내다 보면 불빛에 얼굴이 벌겋게 달아오른다 불안에 젖은 풍경을 쉽게 들키지 않는 벽난로 옆 나무 탁자에서

나는 혼자 기다리고 있었다 벽에 걸린 장미도 이제는 새알 대신 전구를 품은 커다란 까치둥지도 빛이 바래 마른 풀냄새가 조금 짙어졌을 뿐, 가수는 여전히 낡은 레코드판 위에서 삼십 년도 더 흐른 옛 사랑을 노래하고

아무 것도 변한 것은 없었다 한쪽 다리가 짧은 맞은편 의자를 삐딱하게 빼놓은 채 잠시 그의 모습을 떠올리고 달곰했던 목소리를 기억하며 두 개의 각설탕을 털어 넣은 커피로 역류하는 추억을 다독이며

나이프를 들고 여물지 않은 상처 속에 잘 숙성된 함박스테이크를 꾸역꾸역 밀어 넣었다 낮은 음계로 떠돌던 한 쌍의 낯선 목소리가 온전히 장작불 속으로 사그라질 때까지

문은 열리지 않았다 간혹 뒤늦게 도착한 새들이 창가에 와서 흐린 불빛에 길을 묻고 있었을 뿐

* 카페 포크웨이즈: 김포시 고촌면에 있는 카페

POME
김경식
《스토리문학》수필등단
계간《다시올문학》시 등단
수필집『마음의 걸린 풍경 하나』

The Producer ID

Gim Gyeong-gon

The first snow storm in a decade
has collapsed the penhouse.
The yard fowls remained calm
as they were taken out of the debris.

I plop down
only after I send out the surviving fowls.
I order a roast chicken and drink bear,
watching a live TV report on an earthquake.
On the plate a torn chicken prostrates.
I read departure on the chicken' s back.
Neat narcotic drugs called drinks are cheap and
abundant.
Plucking the legs resembling clay cake,
I shed my shameful puerility.
My shame is scorched by fire
and I miss my glass in a flash.
My neck stomachs the vegetable pickles
over a cynical glass.
The raw wing pricks its feathers.
The splinters of bone and the hooded chicken.
The flesh is salvaged from
the dismembered chicken.

A sheet of paper
among the wreckages and debris.
The producer ID No. 13432596
lies there frozen.

생산자이력제

김 경 곤

십년 만에 폭설이 내려 닭장을 주저앉혔다
쓰러진 잔해 속에서 꺼내는 닭은 평온했다
간간히 살아남은 닭을 출하하고서야 나도 주저앉는다

통닭을 주문하고 술을 마신다
티브이 속 실시간으로 지진사태 중계를 보며
접시에는 할복한 닭이 엎드려 있다
닭의 등으로 이별을 읽는다
술이라는 깔끔한 마취제는 싸고도 흔하지
진흙과자 같은 다리를 뜯어 마리 수 늘리며
이젠 구질구질한 치기는 구겨 넣자
불에 덴 듯 부끄러움은 마취되고
발화스위치처럼 툭 술잔을 놓친다
냉소적인 술잔 넘어 깍두기를 먹고 있는 모가지,
생경한 날개가 솟대처럼 깃털을 세운다
허벅지를 밟아대는 뼛조각, 사고의 폭은 축소되고
후드를 뒤집어 쓴 통닭에 삼지창을 들이 민다
해체된 통닭의 밀어 속에서 구출해 낸 살덩이,
터벅터벅 마취된 통닭의 꼬인 발자국 따라
시선 끌고 간 쓰레기장에 의기소침함이 앉아 있다

다 버리고 자리에 앉자 잔해더미 속의 종이 한 장
퍼즐 같은 생산자이력제 식별번호 13432576,
소리 없이 얼어붙었다

POME

김경곤
《농민문학상》 시부문 우수상
연천문인협회 부회장역임, 다시올문학 편집인
시산맥상 수상
시집 『황동부전나비의 비상』

The Life in the Field That Has Stumbled

Gim Yeung-eun

I went out to greet the spring
Following the season that turned around
To survive the winter
As if you'd turn out a visitor

Into the street
Where it rained.

The pattering sound that broke the silence;
When I looked at the place
That would turn green endlessly,
The yellow field that has stumbled by surprise
Startled up helter-skelter,
Racing into the rain.

I must hurry up.

One doesn't perceive or capture the spring's speed
With that unmeasurable speed
It is pouring down from the sky.

Embracing the seasons of endurance
The jaundiced field
And other seasons that seep in
Are waking up with a radiant presence.

자빠진 들판에 생명이

김영은

나그네 등 떠밀어 거리로 내몰듯
겨울을 보내고자
돌아서는 세월 앞세워
봄을 만나러 갔지

비 내리는 거리로

후두 둑 정적을 깨는 소리
끝없이 푸르러질 그곳 바라보니
놀라 자빠진 누런 들판이
황급히 자리 털고
빗속으로 달려가는데

서둘러야 한다

봄의 속도는 알 수 없기에 붙잡을 수 없듯
그렇게 잴 수 없는 속도로
하늘에서 쏟아져 내리고 있다

인고의 세월을 품고
황달걸린 들판과
스며드는 다른 계절이
환한 기적으로 깨나고 있다

POME
김영은
2003년 월간 《시사문단》 등단, 공동시집 『어떤초상화의 모티부』
다시올문학 발행인, 도서출판 다시올 대표
maxim3515@naver.com

Poems of 100 Major Contemporary Korean Poets

Poems of 100 Major Contemporary Korean Poets
한국 대표 100인 영역시선

초판인쇄 2013년 5월 20일
초판발행 2013년 5월 25일

지은이 | 고창수 역
발행인 | 김영은
디자인 | 송동현 박지혜
펴낸곳 | 다시올
출판등록 | 제 310-2007-00028

우편 | 139-050
주소 | 서울 노원구 월계동 382-55(중앙빌 2동 1호)
전화 | 070-7431-5941
팩스 | 031-855-5941
메일 | maxim3515@naver.com

ISBN 978-89-94414-39-3 93800

정가 15,000원

*파본은 본사나 구입하신 서점에서 교환해 드립니다.